C000185264

THE 1ST HOUSEHOLD CAVALRY 1943–44

ALSO BY GARRY O'CONNOR

The Pursuit of Perfection: A Life of Maggie Teyte
Ralph Richardson: An Actor's Life
Darlings of the Gods: One Year in the Lives of Laurence Olivier and Vivien
    Leigh
Olivier: In Celebration (editor)
Sean O'Casey: A Life
William Shakespeare: A Life
Alec Guinness: Master of Disguise
The Secret Woman: A Life of Peggy Ashcroft
William Shakespeare: A Popular Life
Paul Scofield: The Biography
Alec Guinness, the Unknown: A Life
Universal Father: A Life of John Paul II
The Darlings of Downing Street: The Psychosexual Drama of Power

FICTION

Darlings of the Gods
Campion's Ghost: The Sacred and Profane Memories of John Donne, Poet
Chaucer's Triumph

DRAMA

Different Circumstances
Dialogue Between Friends
Debussy Was My Grandfather, Two Plays

THEATRE AND CINEMA STUDIES

Le Théâtre en Grande-Bretagne
French Theatre Today
The Mahabharata: Peter Brook's Epic in the Making

THE 1ST HOUSEHOLD CAVALRY 1943–44

IN THE SHADOW OF MONTE AMARO

GARRY O'CONNOR

Taken from the war diaries of 1HCR officers

Research by Victoria Ewart

DEDICATION

To the memory of John Ewart, and to all Household Cavalry men, past and present

The history of a battle is not unlike the history of a ball. Some individuals may recollect all the little events of which the great result is the battle won or lost, but no individual can recollect the order in which, or the exact moment at which, they occurred, which makes all the difference as to their value or importance.

Arthur Wellesley, 1st Duke of Wellington

First published 2013
by Spellmount, an imprint of
The History Press
The Mill, Brimscombe Port
Stroud, Gloucestershire, GL5 2QG
www.thehistorypress.co.uk

© Garry O'Connor, 2013

The right of Garry O'Connor, to be identified as the Author
of this work has been asserted in accordance with the
Copyrights, Designs and Patents Act 1988.

All rights reserved. No part of this book may be reprinted
or reproduced or utilised in any form or by any electronic,
mechanical or other means, now known or hereafter invented,
including photocopying and recording, or in any information
storage or retrieval system, without the permission in writing
from the Publishers.

British Library Cataloguing in Publication Data.
A catalogue record for this book is available from the British Library.

ISBN 978 0 7524 8857 8

Typesetting and origination by The History Press
Printed in Great Britain

CONTENTS

FOREWORD

by His Grace The Duke of Wellington KG, LVO, OBE, MC, DL

This book pays fitting tribute to the surviving officers and men, to those no longer with us, and indeed all members of the Household Cavalry Regiment, for the values and traditions it celebrates. Full of vivid detail and humour, it will appeal to everyone interested in war and conflict, to serving personnel the world over, but also to those keen to read accounts of the British Army in Italy in World War Two. I was commissioned as a second lieutenant (or Cornet) in the Royal Horse Guards in 1940 and served in the First Household Cavalry Regiment during the African and European campaigns. I am delighted that the book includes my own contribution, and I was fascinated to read for the first time the diaries and accounts of my fellow officers of our engagement in the Italian campaign of 1943–1944. I had no idea such vivid records were being made on a daily basis. The book binds together material from these diaries, interviews with the author, official and historical accounts and personal letters to home, and shapes a gripping narrative of the campaign we fought through ravaged and starving Italy, which had in 1943 changed sides, and was then subjected to cruel and savage Nazi reprisal. Here, therefore, largely told and taken from the mouths and recorded words of the few survivors who are in their nineties, among which I figure, as well as those who have gone, is the chance to share again our youthful adventures in the line, our hazards and tribulations, and gain insight into why such a war should never be fought again.

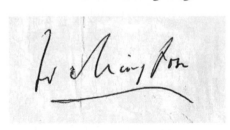

ABBREVIATIONS

1HCR	1st Household Cavalry Regiment
2i/c	Second in command
AA /Ack Ack	Anti aircraft
A/C	Armoured Car
ADC	Aide de Camp
AEC	Army Education Centre
AOC	Air Officer Commanding
AOC	Air Operations Centre
APM	Assistant Provost Marshal
AP	Armour Piercing
AT	Anti tank
Carp L	Carpathian Lancers
CB	Counter Battery
CIH	Central India Horse
CMOs	commanders
CO	Commanding Officer
COH/CoH	Corporal of Horse
COH	Corporal of the Horse
COMNS	Communications
Cpl	Corporal
Det Pol Eng.	Polish Engineers
DF	Directed Fire
DIV	division
DPO	Divisional post office

FA	Field Artillery
FANY	First Aid Nursing Yeomanry
GHQ	General Headquarters
GSO	General Staff Officer
Infm	information
IO	Intelligence Officer
LAD	Light Aid Detachment officer
LG	The Life Guards
MC	Medical Corps
MG	Machine gun
MP	Machine pistol
MO	Medical Officer
MP	Machine pistol
MP	Military Police
NCO	Non Commissioned Officer
OP	Observation Post
PW	prisoner of war
POW	prisoner of war
RCM	Regimental Corporal Major
RSM	Regimental Sergeant Major
Recce	Reconnaissance
REME	Royal Electrical and Mechanical Engineers
RHG	Royal Horse Guards
RHQ	Regimental Headquarters
RQCM	Regimental Quartermaster Corporal Major
SCM	Squadron Corporal Major
SO	Signals Officer
Sqn Ldrs	Squadron Leaders
Tp	Troop
Tpr	Trooper
TSMG	Thompson Sub machine Gun
UC	Unclassified
WO	Wireless Operator
WT	Wireless telegraph
YR	Yeomanry Regiment

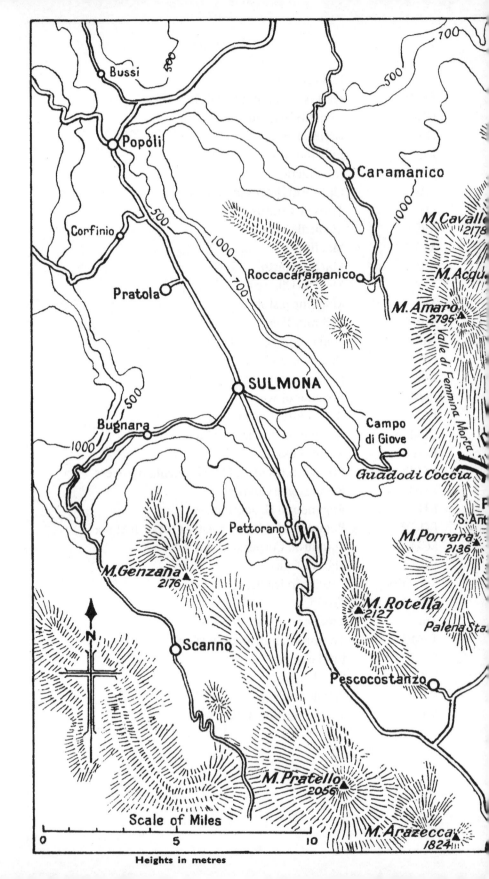

Bussi

Popoli

Caramanico

M. Cavall
2178

Corfinio

M. Acqu

Pratola

Roccacaramanico

M. Amaro
2795

Valle di Femmina Morta

SULMONA

Campo
di Giove

Bugnara

Guado di Coccia

S. Ant

Pettorano

M. Porrara
2136

M. Genzana
2176

M. Rotella
2127

Palena Sta.

N

Scanno

Pescocostanzo

M. Pratello
2056

Scale of Miles

0   5   10

M. Arazecca
1824

Heights in metres

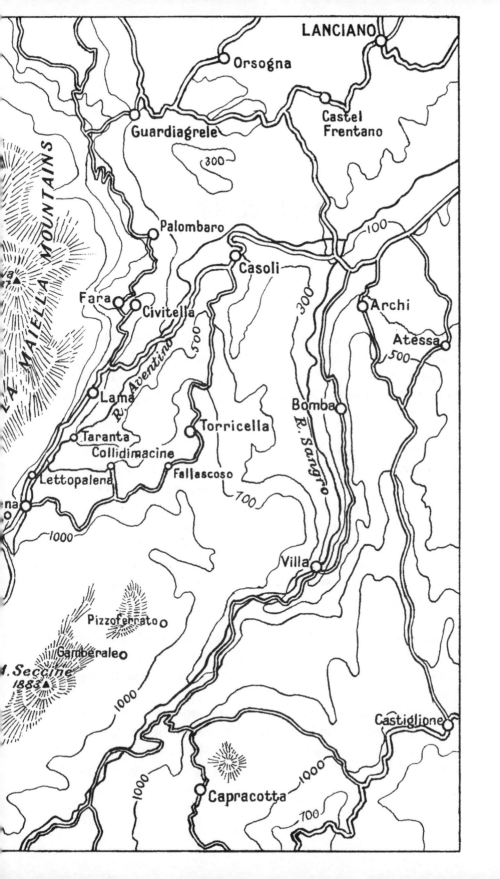

INTRODUCTION

Nothing better sets the scene for the Second World War probing and pursuit, reconnaissance role of the 1st Household Cavalry Regiment, a composite of the Horse Guards and the Blues and Royals – the British Army's two most senior regiments – than this entry in Lieutenant M.H.A. Fraser's diary:

> *May 8, 9, 1944.* The Bosch really are devils. I was one of the first patrols to enter Palena after the Bosch left it on the night of May 7th/8th so found it almost exactly as they left it. About 80% of houses are useless, many have walls standing but others also are completely flat. Much of this is due to shelling, but before they left the Germans blew up many of them with mines. The mess inside the houses is terrible. It looked just as if the Germans had walked into them, turned everything upside down, taken everything they wanted and then pushed off. Several houses reek of dead bodies under the rubble.

The Germans, tenaciously defending from the heights of *Monte Amaro,* or Bitter Mountain, of the Maiella Range in central Italy, had not gone far, and were to make it as uncomfortable as they could to stop the Regiment moving forward.

Previous to landing at Naples, the Regiment had since late 1943 been leisurely encamped in Egypt in the heat of the desert, training and taking part in mock battles. In April 1944 it embarked to go into the line in the inhospitable Apennines, where, advancing through the 'scorched earth' of the German retreat, it had to abandon its armoured cars and proceed on foot.

The Regiment became caught up in a very different type of conflict than in its earlier engagements, and these now involved civilians and townships, and a largely unseen enemy. The aim of the following pages is to show what this conflict was, and how the officers of the Regiment magnificently fulfilled their duty while observing the highest rules of behaviour and commitment,

Hearing them talk in their own words, we get under the skin of these young officers, learn what their characters are, where they come from, how they look, speak, act – and how they feel about the death of their comrades, the dangers they face, and the conditions they live through. Their insights and dramas multiply in depth and interest. They inhabit a very small corner of the total war, a very personal one, full of charm and humour, yet they are in the shadow of untold horror and destruction. Even here, they find unexpected touches of comradeship and coincidence – as well as danger.

Compared to the mass engagement and carnage of millions in the various theatres of the Second World War the account is very human and personal. They are generally cheerful and genial figures, from 'Wispy', their Commanding Officer, down through the ranks: as 'Porchey' (Lord Porchester) says of John Ewart, he 'is laughing as usual'– 'Happy Warriors', as Evelyn Waugh subtitled his *Officers and Gentlemen*. We discover and engage with them at a moment just before the tipping point of the war, both in Italy and Europe at large, leading to victory.

To the end this cohesive unit, in the midst of the chaos and uncertainty of war, strives to preserve its curious, not to say eccentric but certainly unique, identity.

First, by way of introduction, is a curious and heartening tale, which is more than tinged with sadness: that of how I came to be involved in this project, to begin with by listening to the memories the officers had to share with me; and second, by reading the tens of thousands of words of their accounts and diaries, with a view to thinking how a book could be made out of them that might appeal not only to serving and former officers and men of the Regiment, but also to members of the armed services generally, and readers interested in 'living history' from the last survivors of the Second World War.

John Ewart was one of the very young lieutenants involved, and until he died at the age of 87 on September 6, 2012, a landowner and businessman residing just outside King's Sutton on the Northamptonshire–Oxfordshire border where I live with my wife Vicky and family. While Vicky and I had met John many times socially, he was of our parents' generation, and was a man of many interests; businessman, farmer, landowner, and long-standing County Councillor, as well as keen foxhunter and yachtsman. He was very patriotic, a Tory and a devout Roman Catholic who regularly attended the local Catholic Mass in our beautiful Anglican church in the village.

John had always been an avid reader, especially of biographies, history and books about politics, and had read several of my works. In his mid-eighties he had given up hunting and sold his estate in Devon and lived permanently at Astrop House, his Georgian manor with grounds designed by Capability Brown, which he bought in 1952.

One day he invited Vicky and me, his daughter Lavinia and Charles, her husband, and his niece Victoria, a researcher, to dinner to meet two more ex-lieutenants of his age, Herbert du Plessis and Malcolm Fraser, who served with him in the 1st Household Cavalry Regiment in 1943–44. All three, we had been briefed earlier, had kept diaries during that period, although, for the reason that they might fall into enemy hands and give away vital intelligence, such a practice was forbidden under military law. If discovered the diarists could have been arrested and tried by court martial.

Herbert and Malcolm, as well as John, exchanged with us fascinating memories of that campaign and subsequently I received Malcolm's diary, which had been transcribed, as well as a memoir by Herbert based on his own diary. John was very keen to know what I thought of the material and if I could make a book out of it. He had meantime amassed a challenging and far-ranging collection of books about the Regiment and the Italian campaign from the time he joined until the end of the European war in May 1945, as well as regimental memorabilia and histories.

We then set out, with Victoria his niece doing the research, to see if any of the other young officers at the time who were in HCR – and especially in 1st or A Squadron – had written diaries or letters, or were still alive and would be happy to be interviewed. Victoria tracked down addresses of those few more who were still with us, or, if deceased, their relatives, to ask if there might be any material we could draw on.

John, Victoria, and I held frequent meetings to discuss the project and we soon amassed, in the farm office at Walton Grounds, King's Sutton, a veritable treasure, a rare enclave of living history, which had not been brought to public view before.

I still felt unsure how to approach and shape the material we had gathered. John was most reluctant at first to have his own diary, which he kept only from joining the Regiment up to October 1944, typed by his devoted secretary, Heather Rawden, and it was only after repeated requests that he consented.

By extraordinary coincidence, three more diaries concentrating just on that one year came unexpectedly to light after I had written the synopsis. The first was that of Lieutenant John Shaw, suggested to me by Lieutenant-General Sir Barney White-Spunner, author of *Horse Guards*, his magnificent account of The Life Guards and The Blues and Royals. The second was the prison diary of Ian Van Ammel, whom I interviewed before his death in July 2012. The third, that of Gavin Astor, came our way only at the very last moment, in November 2012, by when the book was well underway.

In addition, His Grace The Duke of Wellington, then Captain Marquess Douro, generously provided a written account of his earlier desert campaigns and agreed to be interviewed. I also interviewed the Marquess of Anglesey, then Lieutenant Earl of Uxbridge.

I cannot do justice to the unflagging and generous enthusiasm of John Ewart, who drew on a wide network of friends and colleagues and put heart and soul into the creation of this book. It was very much his book from the beginning, from his approval of the synopsis and his dedicated overseeing of all stages as it progressed, until the time of his death in early September. All during the winter of 2011–12 he was in and out of hospital, and it was touch and go whether he would survive until the summer. Even so, he was determined that the book should be written, and overjoyed when we found a publisher in The History Press. His next concern was the launch of the book, for which an unbelievable amount of organisation was mustered even before I began to write.

He was always very concerned that I should have complete freedom with the material and take any liberties that I might want to make it engaging and appeal to the widest possible readership. Quite often I would answer when he queried something he feared might be a bit risqué, 'We can't leave that bit out, it's what will help sales' – while of course I was not entirely sure I was right, but he trusted my instinct and experience. And what he wanted, being a businessman, was for the book to sell as many copies as possible. He would ask, 'How many copies are going to be printed?'– again even before I'd started.

I must emphasise that this is wholly my own work, in that I must be held responsible for the choices of inclusion or omission and the errors, judgments and opinions that are to be found here. Victoria Ewart and I have done our best to ensure factual accuracy, to respect copyright, and consult those whose material we have drawn on, or interviewed, and obtain permissions where necessary. There are acknowledgements as well as a bibliography at the end of the book.

I was very glad that I could show to John in rough form the work in progress only a fortnight before he died, and he was able to browse through and enjoy it for several hours. I believe he was very happy knowing that it would be finished – in time for the launch!

To him therefore my heartfelt thanks, and hopes that this book fulfils his dream and expectation, and embodies his warmth, his love of life and generosity, his honesty, and – one thing utterly out of date today – his modesty.

I have generally kept to the original spellings, punctuation and vocabulary, changing them only when they might result in misunder-standing or obscurity.

CHAPTER ONE

PRELUDE – THE TERRIBLE SAGA OF THE DEATH OF CAVALRY HORSES

In World War II it usually took months to go to and come back from war. Today a soldier can go out on patrol and kill someone or have one of his friends killed and call his girlfriend on his cell phone that night and probably talk about anything except what just happened.

Karl Marlantes, *What it is like to go to war*

The composite regiment of Life Guards and Blues, now called 1st Household Cavalry Regiment, had set out with its horses to Palestine in January 1940 travelling across France through Marseilles and then crossing the Mediterranean, during which the horses 'had a miserable time and suffered very badly', according to the Duke of Wellington in conversation with the author, then listed in records as plain Lieutenant A.V. Wellesley, and known among his circle as Valerian. 'This was the last time horses were ever used in the British Army.'

The horses – quite extraordinary to think in this day and age – but in 1939 we had three regular regiments of cavalry with horses and eight yeomanry regiments, I believe about 10,000 horses and 15,000 men. The Greys and Royals were already in Palestine. This was the time of the Arab rebellion, and they had done very well in the operations particularly in the rural areas and it was felt if we were going to use cavalry at all it would be best to send them to the Middle East. They decided in May or April the Regiment, plus the remains of the rest of the cavalry regiments less the

Greys and Royals who were already in Palestine, and all the horse yeomanry regiments, should go to the Middle East. They left via France from
Marseilles and landed in Palestine.

They were optimistic the war would last a short while before they went.
This was 1940, the 'phoney war', and there had been no engagement
with the Nazis. They did not think they might never see their sweet-
hearts or families again, and even if at the back of their minds there
were fears, they did not dwell on them.

Aged 25, Lt Wellesley, was a young man of gentle aspect but as
you might expect from the great-great-grandson of the General who
had beaten Napoleon, was not given to morbidity or introspection.
Wellesley was third in line to the title of Duke. Like his illustrious ancestor he would speak his mind directly.

I sense at once in his presence seventy-two years later, when he was
97, an awareness of the cost of war, perhaps echoing the former Duke
who said, 'Well I thank God! I don't know what it is to lose a battle, but
certainly nothing can be more painful than to gain one with the loss of
so many of one's friends.' His Grace's own similar words are 'Every day
we had to deal with what came our way, and we didn't stop to dwell on
our problems. You were never sure what would happen the next day,
which of your friends would be gone, forever. It was all part of the job.'

Valerian Wellesley did not travel out with the horses. He went two
or three months later, with the first reinforcements. He took a draft of
37 men on the *Empress of Britain* from Liverpool. They sailed over two
months to get to the Near East because by that time the submarines
were very active.

> The great thing about the *Empress* was that she was equipped for leisure
> cruises before the war so whisky was 1d a glass, and it was far from being
> 'dry'. We had around 2-3000 men – reinforcements for all the regiments
> out there, not just the cavalry. We sailed out into the Atlantic and virtu-
> ally across to the West Indies, and returned and came back to Freetown
> on the West Coast of Africa where we refueled.

Lt Wellesley was in charge of the guard policing the vessel, whose pas-
sengers included 50 Queen Alexandra nurses, 'No improper behaviour
on the deck – or in the lifeboats' was his responsibility, which meant,

'I couldn't get up to anything myself.' No one was allowed ashore here, but the *Empress* was solicited by hawkers on little native boats in the harbour peddling sex and combustibles.

> East now into the South Atlantic, docking at Cape Town, where everyone went ashore. The people in Cape Town were wonderful to us, and we spent 3 or 4 days there. There was an elderly cavalry captain from WW1, who was ship's commandant, who said to me, 'Look I want you to go and liaise with the Cape Town police and go round all the night spots and make sure no one is left behind because we have to sail at 5am tomorrow morning.' So I did this and had to visit every brothel and club with the Cape Town police who were quite a tough lot. As a young officer I was rather shocked by some of the behaviour. I reported back to my ship's commandant at about midnight and said I couldn't find anyone, so he said well done, everyone was on board, and we sailed up through the Suez Canal to Port Said. It was pretty awful in the Indian Ocean, incredibly hot and before the days of air conditioning. Just one man died of heat stroke – maybe two. Then from Port Said we went by train up to the Regiment.

Wellesley took his thirty-plus intake to Tulkara where 1HCR had its base. On the night of arrival his Squadron Leader arranged a little 'welcome' party. They were having dinner at a long table in the open air when 'suddenly there was a lot of firing and it seemed as if we were being ambushed.' High jinks abounded: they were part of the ethos, so they got their own back on the commander by lacing his gin with a chemical that turned his urine bright green.

Valerian shot duck on Lake Haleh, later drained by the Israelis but then inhabited by a race of Arabs said to have webbed feet and to be immune to malaria. He took part in exercises. 'I was in a Forward OP when the rest of the Regiment was in the Jordan valley, Plain of Esdraelun, a resounding Biblical name. The whole of the 4th Cavalry Brigade, which included 2000 horses, advanced as an exercise. I watched this enormous force advance and charge – such an amazing sight which never happened again, for this was the last of the great cavalry exercises.'

Early in 1941, Valerian, who had patrolled on horseback, heard they were to be mechanized, and that all the horses over 15 years old were to be put down in our camp areas and the remainder would be sent to horse transport companies in Egypt. Later, many went to Greece for the campaign there and were lost to the Germans. In December at Beisan in the Jordan Valley he was told they were to be issued with wooden-bodied Morris 15 hundredweight trucks – an armoured car regiment without the armour – so functioning, as they were to in Iraq and Syria, as motorised infantry.

> The tactics were not easy to define. When our horses left us we were told our future role was that of an Armoured Car Regiment – a role we welcomed. In general terms the main role of our A/Cs is armoured reconnaissance. Assuming that a formation such as a division is advancing in a mobile operation, it will be preceded by an A/C formation whose duty is to cover and protect forward units, report on enemy movement, probe for weak spots in enemy defences and if possible push aside enemy forward units. In a static situation an A/C Regiment's main task is forward observation to give early warning of enemy movement and intentions. In a withdrawal an A/C Regiment may be asked to cover withdrawal of, say, our own infantry, or other formations and delay and harass forward enemy movement.

On one especially sad and gruelling day, Valerian had to separate the horses which were older than fifteen from the others.

> We shot them with a revolver or with a humane killer with a bullet in it. You drew a line from the ear to the eye and where it met that is where you put the bullet. The bullet in this case was either from a pistol or a humane killer. I think I used my pistol because there were not enough humane killers around.
>
> It was a horrible business I had to do with 14 old horses in my troop. Those lovely old black horses had taken part in all the great state occasions of the last ten years, including the 1936 Coronation. There on a bleak Palestinian hill they were left to be eaten by wolves and jackals. As I look back it was one of the most horrible moments of my life.
>
> Then we spent that winter in Beisan in the Jordan valley until February, when we got these ancient and wooden-bodied Morris trucks and we did our best to do manoeuvres. Suddenly we were on a big exercise. The Germans had managed to infiltrate a certain Dr Grobba into Iraq and he effected a coup d'état in which Raschid Ali, a pro-German soldier, took over, and suddenly the British Government woke up to the

fact that in Iraq they had a hostile regime who no doubt could be a great nuisance to us with regard to our position in the Middle East, and also astride oil reserves, so they looked around and couldn't find anyone to send over apart from the 4th Cavalry Brigade that was in the Jordan Valley. Everyone thought at the time, even the legendary leader Colonel Glubb Pasha, that British power in the Middle East was about to collapse. The first target of the Axis plan was the tactically important RAF base at Habbaniya, where flying boats from England used to land on their way to India.

The base was a huge complex of power plants, workshops, water supplies, native cantonments and armed services and civilian messes that had cost millions — a self-supporting town of over 10,000 inhabitants, of which 2,200 were fighting men. Built by British contractors in the desolate Iraqi desert next to a huge and choppy expanse of water, with streets named Kingsway and Cheapside, and even a Piccadilly Circus, in March 1941 its garrison faced the 9,000 men and 50 guns of Raschid Ali's besieging army.

> They decided to send us across the desert to Iraq to relieve the base where British families had fled from Baghdad, where hundreds of these subjects had earlier taken refuge. The first thing the renegade force did was to try and take over the base, which they failed to do, as the RAF levies were very gutsy, showed complete contempt for danger under fire, and fought them off. We were dispatched in our wooden trucks across the desert to relieve the siege.

The levies, locally raised forces, mainly Assyrians but also Kurds and Yazideees, were fanatically pro-British, and worshipped the King and Queen. They lived in small huts, performed war dances and each had an average of six children. The Germans had use of airfields in Syria, which was occupied by French Vichy troops fighting on the German side. The forced 'march' to relieve the garrison was unforgettable.

> The searing heat of well over 100°F in the shade seemed to bounce off the black volcanic rock which covered much of the desert and, combined with clouds of dust and a shortage of water, made this journey in old open 15 cwt Morris trucks a pretty testing one. To my considerable

annoyance my dark glasses blew off in a sandstorm, which to begin with caused me great discomfort.

Our daily ration of water for the journey for six men was approximately one gallon. These were carried in Chargules, which were canvas bags that theoretically allowed a small amount of water to evaporate and this kept the contents cool when hung from the side of the truck. Initially we didn't think much of them as they leaked quite a lot but our old line cavalry reservists, who had served in India, assured us that when covered in mud and sand they worked quite well. This proved to be the case as they got a coating of sand as we drove along in clouds of dust.

They travelled for four days at something like a hundred miles a day until they reached Rutbah Wells inside Iraq and within striking distance of Habbaniya and Baghdad. Here they were bombed ineffectually by a single German ME 110 fighter-bomber, living proof that the Germans were using bases in Iraq and Syria.

One evening Valerian spotted several coveys of sand grouse, flying into a water hole: 'So I dug out the 16 bore gun I carried throughout the war in a saddle holster, and made my way there. I managed to shoot a brace, which I carried back in triumph intending to have them for breakfast. Alas, such was the heat they were putrid by the morning. I should have gutted them immediately.'

On the way, at Mafraq, the force was joined by Colonel Glubb Pasha's Arab Legion, provided by King Abdullah to support the British. As Wellesley stood watching refugees with their household goods and livestock coming in a steady stream down the road from Baghdad, a voice at his elbow said, 'Sad sight, isn't it?'

Beside me stood a short man in khaki drill with medal ribbons and impressive badges of rank with which I was not familiar. He had a pronounced cleft in his chin and on his head he wore an Arab Khuffiah. I realised I was talking to the great Glubb Pasha, commander of the Arab Legion.

Behind him was a group of what 1HCR called 'Glubb's girls'. They spoke a while until he moved off into the desert. While memories of Lawrence of Arabia had faded in the Arab world, Glubb was the present legendary figure who hated his sobriquet 'the second Lawrence'. Arabs called him 'the Father of the Little Chin', because his jaw had been partly shot away in the First World War and his teeth had grown together to look like a beak. He was not one to chat, Wellesley noticed, but so revered was Glubb that dozens of Arabs, often sheiks, just liked to spend time in his presence in silence.

The Legion consisted of Bedouin tribesmen from the Badia desert, warriors with black ringlet hair and lean, dark, hawkish faces, who wore long khaki drill-robes festooned with belts of ammunition. Each carried a rifle, an evil-looking dagger and a pistol, while their head-dresses were red-and-white check Khuffiahs.

The Legion's task was to protect the long and open flanks from marauding tribesmen and dissident bands of rebels, notably that led by Fawzi Kawachi, a well equipped force of some 500 men. Fawzi operated with French support from Syria. Fawzi was a well trained leader who had served as an officer in the Turkish army in the Great War and com-manded, as an able tactician, an effective mobile force. He was a cruel and barbaric foe: he poured petrol over his captives and burnt them alive, or stripped them and turned them loose in the desert to die. Fawzi was to prove, Wellesley said, 'a real thorn in my flesh'.

When they arrived in Habbaniya the Regiment found the besieging Iraqis had fled to Baghdad, so there was no resistance. That same night, relief came to the men in the Wadi. Near the lake, Valerian never forgot the sight of 'hundreds of men tearing off the clothes they had been wearing for the best part of a very hot and exhausting week and racing stark naked, like a crowd of excited schoolboys, into the cool waters of the lake'.

The RAF had a troop of old Rolls-Royce engine A/Cs equipped with First World War Vickers machine guns. They were used by the RAF for internal security purposes in the lawless tribal areas of the desert near Habbaniya. This troop during a routine patrol managed to get two armoured cars stuck in soft sand. Fawzi Kawachi and his band captured and removed one of these cars.

A troop of B Squadron 1HCR, sent to recover the other car and rescue the crews, was unable to move it, and Valerian went with his troop with a LAD (light aid detachment recovery vehicle) to get the A/C out and reinforce the B Squadron troop, as Fawzi was expected to return.

Valerian's troop combined with the B Squadron troop to extricate the A/C from the soft sand and took it back to Habbaniya. On their way an RAF Gloucester Gladiator looking for its RAF armoured car, saw them and strafed the recovering party before the pilot realised his mistake, killing a man in B Squadron.

That in Fawzi Kawachi Valerian had an identifiable enemy, a very personal figure who nearly obliterated him, was to be shown not long after, when Fawzi and his dangerous irregulars escaped the fall of Baghdad to the relieving British force and moved to Abu Kemal on the Syrian frontier.

Valerian, with A Squadron under Major Eion Merry, set out in pursuit. Unfortunately, they had none of 'Glubb's girls' with them to decipher intelligence. They had reached the Euphrates from high ground, which squeezed them close to the riverbank, when Valerian looked towards the crest of the hill on his left and saw

> ... a line of perhaps two hundred men outlined against the sky as they crossed; a line of beaters advancing on you! John Shaw's troop was soon exchanging fire with the enemy and since we were on lower ground and heavily outnumbered, Tony – Captain Murray-Smith – gave the order to withdraw back to the vehicles. Before long we were all firing and dropping back by sections. The situation started to look a little ugly as the enemy was pressing down on us as we got nearer the vehicles. We were starting to take the odd casualty. Trooper Martin, who was with Tony, was hit in the leg and there were others not seriously wounded whom I did not see. The last hundred yards was frankly a bit of a scramble and not exactly the cool orderly withdrawal one would have desired. The situation was further exacerbated by the fact that at Squadron HQ the third troop and the vehicles were now under heavy rifle fire from the riverbank. Two vehicles had already been hit and immobilised and had to be put on tow under fire. We held off the enemy for as long as we could and then ran like hell for the trucks and leapt aboard; the whole group of vehicles driving off in reasonable order but at great speed under heavy fire from all sides. Before long we were clear of the danger area in more open country and within a few miles were back in our harbour area in the wide spaces of the desert.

Valerian may well have felt some affinity here with his ancestor ('My grandfather was the first Duke's grandson') and could have remarked that this was 'a near run thing', and with a further comment on Fawzi – 'by God he has bugged me' – uttered just before Napoleon's move from France before Waterloo. (Perhaps I should mention here that it was the first Duke, with his battlefield eye for the ground, who said 'You must build your House of Commons on the river: so ... that the populace cannot exact their demands by sitting down round you.')

Valerian and his troop had pushed as far as, or even into, Syria when on his primitive emergency wireless set (main communication was by key and Morse code) he heard, believing it a regular contact with Squadron HQ, a faint signal asking for his position. It was a mysterious request, and he felt uncomfortable. When he called again the reply, loud and clear, asked again for his position, which made him even more uneasy. Five minutes later he was staring into the desert to the west:

I thought I saw a cloud of dust 'no larger than a man's hand' to borrow a biblical expression. A minute later it was quite clear that it was dust and moving fast in my direction. I told Maxted [his Corporal of Horse] to give the order to prepare to move at short notice. This meant packing up all the kit that had been unloaded and there was much grumbling as 'a brew was nearly ready'. It was not a moment too soon, however. I soon saw that this was no ordinary convoy and was almost certainly Fawzi. There seemed to be about a dozen vehicles headed by one, which was different and seemed higher and a strange shape. The sun was now blazing down and the heat was making good observation very difficult. Objects at a distance had become hard to define and had a distorted, elongated appearance. There was something on the leading vehicle which made it appear much higher than the others. Suddenly the penny dropped. It was an armoured car with a turret and what is more I could now see it was an old type RAF Rolls-Royce armoured car and undoubtedly the one which Fawzi had captured at Habbaniyah. My worst fears were confirmed. We would have to move very quickly indeed if we were not to be caught, the consequences of which were not pleasant to think about. I called Maxted over and told him the form and that we must move at once. He must go as fast as he could without causing a panicky rush along our tracks due east. There was no time to take compass bearings. The other trucks would follow behind with me in the rear to watch the enemy. He was to keep an eye on us behind and if any of the trucks broke down the occupants were to be transferred as quickly as possible and the vehicle abandoned. Finally he was to get the Boyes Anti Tank Rifle unboxed and ready for action. If we were going to have to fight, which I sincerely hoped we weren't, I was damned well going to get the armoured car. I looked back at Fawzi's column. It was now

25

barely a thousand yards away and closing fast. I ran to my truck and we moved off after the others.

They escaped, but only just. Fawzi pursued, and it became clear to Wellesley that the wireless set from the captured RAF A/C had tuned into their frequency. For a time they were level pegging on a parallel course, but Valerian was able to contact Squadron HQ to summon help and after a little while Fawzi dropped back and finally abandoned the pursuit.

In spite of losing their horses to vehicular horsepower the Regiment never lost its affinity with the values of horsemanship. The mechanized Regiment kept the vocabulary of the equestrian, cavalry world, calling garages 'stables', and 'dismounting' from their transport. Many of the officers maintained liveries on their estates and were distinguished huntsmen.

Major Jack Hamilton Russell, writing to his wife before El Alamein in 1943, avoided censorship as he described pre-battle preparation: 'My coat is smart, my top-boots polished, my horse's mane plaited and lovely ... but pushed ... bustling around for gloves and whip. The scent is good, the country the cream ... the whole pack of bitches and dogs and riding out best horses ... I am told there are a nice strong lot of foxes about too.'

The Commanding Officer of the Regiment, Lieutenant Colonel Eric Gooch, was a Master of Hounds. In May 1941, two months after they had changed from horses to armoured cars, Gooch, then a Major, was sent on patrol to capture Dr Grobba, the German Minister fomenting trouble among the tribes in Iraq and Syria. He used hunting terms in code to Major-General J.G.W. Clarke. The mission was called 'Grafton' after the hunt, and messages ran 'Made twenty miles point on stale line, covert blank, hounds unable to draw covert satisfactorily, owing to very thick briar. Local inhabitant reports fox leaving covert day before.' Grobba, the fox, got clean away.

One officer later became Equerry to the late Queen Mother, while Lieutenant Lord Porchester, later the 7th Earl of Carnarvon, was from 1969 the Queen's Racing Manager. Many of the NCOs and other ranks joined from the staff of big estates, or were in service to the aristocracy: chauffeurs, sons of estate managers, grooms, household staff, game-keepers, cooks and so on, encouraged to join the Regiment by their masters, and indeed to go on working for them as their 'manservants' (typically they eschew the general army term 'batman').

Porchester writes to his father from Italy, 'I have now got Hemmings, Gavin Astor's [future Lord Astor of Hever] servant as mine [Astor had gone missing, believed dead], he is a proper servant, a footman in peacetime. This regiment after the war will definitely be a source of servants and footmen and grooms, if you want any tell me and I know several who I could get I fancy.'

What makes the Household Cavalry Regiment special is this traditional relationship with the horse, entailing the responsibility, skill and courage that successful horse management and horsemanship requires.

CHAPTER TWO

DRAMATIS PERSONAE
– OUR MAIN WITNESSES

Attitude seems to me to be a parameter which restricts not only our relationships but also our creative efforts.

Sydney Jary, *18 Platoon*

In October 1943 the First Household Cavalry Regiment consists of three Squadrons, A, B and C, and Headquarters, or HQ. Some officers have been serving since the beginning of the war; some of the younger officers have only recently joined prior to October 1943 (see Appendix for the list of officers who served in Italy).

In A Squadron, the RHG, the officers that feature most in these pages are Major Tony Murray-Smith, the Squadron Leader, Captain Marquess Douro, 2i/c (formerly Wellesley, but since the death of his cousin Morny at Salerno, now second in line to the Dukedom); Lieutenants John Shaw, Herbert du Plessis, the Wireless Officer, and Lieutenants Laurence Rook, Ian Van Ammel, John Ewart, Malcolm Fraser, and Gavin Astor, the Intelligence Officer.

In the other squadrons the following are often mentioned: Major Ferris St George, Captain Roddy (Lord) Pratt, Captain Neil Foster, Captain de Piava Raposo, Lts Guy Routledge, Michael Tree, Teddy Lambton, Robin Tudsbery, Kenneth Diacre, John Greenish, Dennis Domvile, Lord Porchester, (Count) Domski Revertera, the Hon. Ned Carson, Malby Crofton, and Henry, Earl of Uxbridge.

Of these the main diarists and interviewees are Douro, Ewart, Shaw, du Plessis, Van Ammel, Fraser and Astor.

Lord Porchester (RHG), C Squadron, is a main contributor by way of the letters he wrote home to Highclere, which he compiled and published as a volume much later. Porchester, generally known as Porchey, grandson of Egyptologist Lord Carnarvon, son of Henry, the 6th Earl, owner of Highclere, was educated at Eton and enlisted at the age of nineteen:

> David Burghesh [later Earl of Westmoreland], Lord Rupert Nevill, John Ewart and I all joined the Household Cavalry at Acton recruiting office on the same day, and were sent to Combermere Barracks, Windsor, and to potential officers squad at Caterham with the 14th company Grenadier Guards, then to armoured car training at Pirbright with the Scots Guards, and finally, Sandhurst.

He befriended Ewart at once, as they both had a love of riding and horses. He took, it seems, quite a bit of money off Ewart at bridge, at any rate at first. He left no diary but wrote loquacious and colourful letters naming everyone he possibly could, to his mother and father, who were divorced, his sister, friends, and Highclere staff. Strong-featured, resembling his father, affectionate and forthright in his letters, even sometimes pugnacious as befits a member of the Eton boxing team, and with a close eye for detail, he sets the scene for his departure:

> I had a ride round the Estate with my father who gave me every sort of advice for active service, including keeping my head down and remembering 'a live subaltern is better than a dead VC'. He also handed me 2 or 3 letters of introduction to friends of his from his race riding days in Cairo. I said farewell to all the estate staff and returned to Windsor. I collected my sun compass, a smart service dress from Major Alan Stanley which fitted me well and a 12 bore shotgun given to me by H C Armstrong, [author of *Grey Wolf*, a biography of Mustapha Kemal], who lived on the estate. Together with other reinforcements and my .22 rifle, which I still have, we left Gooroch for the Middle East on the troopship, *Leopoldville*, a liner which used to do a pre-war run from Antwerp to the Belgian Congo. There were several submarine alerts and much drill, but the worst of the journey to Egypt was being foolish enough to take part in a boxing

competition where I was matched against a sergeant in the Royal Irish
Fusiliers who I later discovered was a welterweight army champion.
I only lasted one and a half rounds before the fight was stopped!

When we finally arrived at Abissaia Barracks, we were met by Captain
Lord Roderic Pratt and Major Gwyn Morgan Jones, who was APM Cairo.

John Ewart (RHG), Troop Leader A Squadron, comes into the Regiment
direct from Beaumont, the Jesuit boarding school, also at the age of
nineteen. At school he had been a brilliant show jumper. His father was
a City businessman who lived and worked in China for a while, where
one of his two sisters was born. After the army he took over and ran his
family trading firm. Later he was Chairman and Managing Director of
a multi-million-pound company, and then became a landowner on the
Oxfordshire–Northamptonshire border: 'When we joined the Regiment
we were interviewed by the Colonel and he just said, "You'll find there
are a lot of people here with lots of money, and a lot of people here with
a small amount of money, but most people will have a bit ... You couldn't
do it for £400 [per annum]".'

Before leaving London for Egypt where 1HCR are based ready in
October 1943 to be moved to the Italian mainland, Ewart confesses his
mind is in a complete whirl because of difficulty in deciding what are
the most important things: religion, home, girls or his two friends ('Ru'
and 'Porchey'). In a very crowded cabin aboard that Belgian ship the
Leopoldville, he is en route to Cairo. The journey via the Atlantic and
Gibraltar is at first very rough:

> Writing this on Monday morning as felt very sick all Sunday. In morning
> I mainly stayed on deck and afternoon and evening slept on bed. Porchey
> was the worst of all. The others pretended they were all right but were
> not really. We went due West having gone North of Ireland. All the men
> except Griffiths were very ill – can't blame them as conditions in the for-
> ward hold where they were are very hard. It made anybody sick to go
> down there.

The days pass in playing bridge (he usually loses): 'Cost of learning to
play bridge – debt'; watching films (*Dangerous Moonlight*); reacting to the
U-boat scares ('dropping of depth charges and sounding of alarms') and
keeping an eye on the coast should they be sunk ('can see the African

coast the whole time so it would not be too far to swim'; and writing to his girlfriend Celia Anson (who is bit too much of a prolific correspondent for him). On arrival at Port Said, Ewart finds 'the usual muddle':

We expected to tie up at 8am so we got up at 6 and were ready by 8. But by this time were still 2 or 3 miles from shore with another convoy in front of us. Had another meal at 10.30 and after a tremendous amount of messing about got in to Port Said at about 2. More messing about trying to find baggage – spent most of my time without success in hold. Eventually found Porchey's trunk. Whilst I was at dinner he found my trunk and later the kit bags in another hold. Bought drinks very cheaply and then took French leave and went ashore with Gunner Commando, Frankie, Dickie, and Teddy. Wandered around and eventually found Porchey with our baggage officially – he had only found one piece but we soon found everything but Porchey's valise and kit bags, which were not yet landed. Returned to ship by lorry – Guard tried to take names ... Must go to bed as up very early to RAC Depot ...

The Regiment was meant to be at Fayid, the military base on the Suez Canal, but when Ewart gets there he finds no one. Someone eventually turns up and he has dinner at the Duty Officer's Club where he meets Gavin Astor, the Regiment's Intelligence Officer, who tells him to be careful with men and NCOs. Astor has already seen drunken sergeant majors fighting. Soon he meets more 1HCR fellow officers who have returned from an exercise:

Saturday. Had breakfast at club – when we returned to camp found some of regiment back from scheme. Paddy Brudenell-Bruce in A Squadron is in the same tent seems very charming, perhaps rather weak. Kenneth Diacre – a Life Guard in C Squadron – a deep character, reads, was at Magdalen Oxford – Malby Crofton, an Eton type, who everybody says is very wet, he seems rather a nonentity. Saw the Colonel [Eric Gooch] with the 2nd in command Iain Merry, Royal Horse Guards, and the Adjutant Ian Henderson. In afternoon saw them singly. – Porchey and me to A (Blue Sqn) Tony Hall and Teddy Noble to C (L.G.) Sqn and Frankie and Dickenson to B (Mixed). Squadron leaders are Tony Murray-Smith A, Foster B, St. George C. Valerian Welleseley is 2nd in command A. After dinner went to bed early. In middle of night woke up by noise and heard

31

> Teddy Lambton, Charlie Mills, and the Signals Officer returning after
> night out – Tent was nearly pulled down.

Ewart is tenaciously aware which officers are Life Guards, and which Blues. Drink is freely available and cheap, and it will be a big temptation when they get to Italy. These officers and their men are not due to be exposed to the grinding battle that develops on the Italian mainland, but more to the cat and mouse game of edging forward in advance of the main forces; watching where and when to pounce, observing when to cut and run, if only temporarily. Essentially, then, they are hunters.

Ewart is short in build, an agile man who moves quickly, with a wide-eyed, boyish look, invariably cheerful and with a smile on his face. He is definitely a newcomer. He at once shows himself – and never stops evaluating the qualities that will make him – a good officer, as well as having his antennae ever attuned to survival. He learns in Egypt to drive a scout car, and one day, driving to the back of a slow-moving column, he misses a gear going downhill. To avoid hitting the one in front he starts overtaking and overtakes the whole column, to his commanding officer's fury, who bans him from driving again.

Lieutenant Herbert du Plessis (RHG), the Wireless Officer. In A Squadron, our main focus in the HCR year, he figures highly. Tall, commanding, with large, almost hawk-like features du Plessis has a deep, sonorous voice. He is a Harrovian with cosmopolitan, aristocratic connections. His father owned – as he was descended from early French settlers – a sugar plantation in Mauritius, which for a time he helped manage. Du Plessis, who boxed at school, already knew Porchey, who was at Eton and in the boxing team. As qualification for this went by weight and not by age, Porchey, at 15 heavy for his years, was unfairly up against boys two years older, and du Plessis has kept a photograph from the Eton/Harrow match of Porchey 'crumbling to his knees on his way down'. (Porchey remains keen throughout his service in organizing and taking part in boxing matches.)

In 1939, du Plessis, aged 17, is in Paris, where his uncle Baron Louis Hauzeur, owner and chief executive of a multinational mining company stretching from Norway through Belgium, France, Spain and North Africa, wants to delay Britain's engagement in the war. To this end, he sends Herbert to persuade his other uncle, Lord Kemsley, owner and editor-in-chief of the *Sunday Times*, to adopt an anti-war policy. Du Plessis:

'Lord Kemsley will see you now Mr du Plessis,' said his secretary with a smile.

A door opened on to an acre of floor space. Already I felt unsure of myself as I started the long walk to the mahogany desk. My mouth was dry.

'Well Herbert what have you been doing in Paris?' said my uncle.

'I have come back with a message for you from Uncle Louis.'

'Is it about that note you translated for him at Deauville?'

'Well, yes.'

The frown over his glasses was not encouraging.

'I am not sure I can listen to you, Herbert. We are at war now. We can't go back can we?'

'Er ... no. But I have to say, the French are not keen on this war at all.'

'That's not what their press says. It's not what their Ambassador says.'

'Um ... no. But in Paris they're very divided. I've talked to a lot of people you know. Monsieur Flandin for instance sends his regards.'

'I remember Flandin very well. What does he say?'

'He says it's very risky and we are not ready, and we should stop it before it's too late. It could be a disaster.'

'But he's in opposition. He's not in the Government.'

'No Sir. But he says the Government itself is very divided on this. Britain has done all the running and France is only following. They feel we should have moved against Hitler a long time back, and now it's too late and he's too strong. We have to rearm properly first.'

'But how is that possible? France is at war, as we are. They can't stop any more than we can.'

'No. But Flandin says that things have changed since the Russian invasion of Poland. At the time, we declared war there was only Germany, a fortnight later Russia marched in, obviously following a secret carve-up. We have declared war on Germany, but not on Russia. No matter what we do we cannot free Poland unless we take on the Soviets.'

'But it's not just about Poland. We have to get rid of Hitler.'

'Yes, sir, but that's another question. The peace lobby says that the war about Poland could be stopped now without dishonour because of the Russian factor. Our forces have not engaged with the Germans yet, so there has been no military defeat. Of course we would lose face for a while. But we would rearm, and be strong. Then Hitler would have to respect us.'

A long pause, and then Lord Kemsley said:

'Look Herbert , you must tell Uncle Louis that I don't make Government policy. I trust my Government to take the right decisions at any given time and my policy is quite simply that I am loyal to my government. I can't listen to this sort of talk at all. Not at all, do you understand?'

The interview was over. He was looking annoyed.

Shortly after, du Plessis joins the Regiment. According to Ewart in his diary, du Plessis was 'an extraordinary person – [he found it] so easy to fall in love both with women and with causes.' He certainly has charisma, and demonstrates strength and independence at an early age.

Lieutenant Ian Van Ammel (RHG), A Squadron. Van Ammel, a year older than Ewart, is originally of Dutch stock, from a family of City merchants and businessman, in whose footsteps he followed after qualifying as a solicitor. He joined the Regiment on a different route, earlier than Lord Porchester, the Earl of Uxbridge and Ewart:

> Six of us went out including du Plessis in August 1942, when we had to go round the Cape in a convoy of reinforcements prior to the battle of El Alamein. We travelled in a dirty little boat from Poland even condemned in World War I. At Alamein I remember our vehicles stuck in the sand in the Qatara depression. The artillery barrage which began the battle lit up the sky ... Then there were thousands of surrendering Italians marching towards us. One threw his packet of pasta at my feet. 'You can have this lot – we never had any water to boil it in!'

When the breakthrough came the Regiment was let loose in pursuit: German officers were reluctant to surrender their pistols – saying they needed them to defend themselves from their men! One, Major Burckhardt, 'a colossal snob, constantly said it was an honour to be taken prisoner by the Household Cavalry'. Ian Van Ammel:

> After Alamein we joined forces with a Yeomanry Regiment of the Ninth Army, which had terrible casualties, and took up positions on the Syrian border with Turkey. I will never forget while we were on exercise in Syria

I said to the driver of my A/C that I would take over for a bit. I climbed in the driver's seat and off we went. We were at a place called Slenfi in the mountains of Lebanon. We were pelting down the mountainside with me at the wheel when a hornet came in, went down my shirt and stung me. I clapped my hands to my stomach, I thought I was going to die. So we went straight back to the place. I said, 'Quick I've been stung by a hornet.' They got some surgical spirit and a wad of cotton wool, gave it a wash and told me to get back to work!

The idea was to invade the soft underbelly of Europe through Albania and Bulgaria, but the Turks wouldn't play ball, so we sat on the Euphrates the whole of that miserable winter – it was a cold nasty miserable winter, then we were sent south again.

When I arrived in the desert the Colonel was Andrew Ferguson. I had come from Cairo to the desert and hadn't met the Colonel until after Alamein. When we were going back a figure climbed down the back of my A/C and I was wearing a black beret and a beautifully embroidered RHG badge, and this voice says 'What is that?' I was startled and realised it was the Colonel. I said it is a badge (stuttering!) He said 'Get rid of it!' So I did not query it. It was old Ferguson, Sarah Ferguson's [the Duchess of York's] grandfather. About two or three months later what happens, forget where we were, up turns the Colonel with a spanking new Life Guards badge. I thought that was a horrible trick – he'd made me get rid of my badge!

Lieutenant Malcolm Fraser (RHG) had no hunting connections, but he joined the Blues as his uncle, Colonel Sir Henry Abel-Smith, commanded the 2nd Household Cavalry Regiment. Fraser, who later became a chartered surveyor, is tellingly descriptive of places and troop movements, much more so than Ewart. At times he could be a fledgling military historian. He loves detail. On his journey out to Port Said he reports on the air action over their massive convoy: 7 troop ships, 6 cargo boats, escorted by 1 battleship and 6 destroyers:

On the evening after passing Algiers we had our first air attack. About 5 or 6 Heinkels came over about a half hour before dusk. It was a lovely evening and you could see them quite plainly. Our air cover consisted of 2 Spitfires, both of which were shot down early in the proceedings! It was great fun watching it and damned exciting. Everything loosed off in the whole convoy, and the noise when our guns went off was terrific. The whole ship shook. The destroyers on our flanks were tugging about all over the place, blazing away madly and I saw quite plainly the bursts from their guns; and the German bombers flying along quite happily well out of range! Waiting to come into the attack.

Anyhow the end of it was that we got three down, and they hit one of our cargo boats slap in the middle, who was on our port stern, some distance away. Clouds of smoke came out of the boat and of course she was left behind – Convoys stop for nobody! But I heard afterwards that she did get into port.

The other attack came two evenings later. This time 14 Huns came over flying very high in perfect formation, and they very nearly got the ship in front of us. They came so low that you could actually see the bomb doors open, and the bombs come out of the plane and come whistling down towards you. Two bombs straddled the ship in front of us, throwing up loads of spray over her, and giving us a hell of a shaking – meanwhile our guns were loosing off in every direction. We had 12 Oerlikons, 4 Bofors, 2 rocket projectors firing 8 at a time, and a 6 pounder on the stern. All these were firing flat out at the same moment. So you can imagine the racket. It was during this barrage that our balloon was shot down by one of our rear Oerlikon gunners!!

The attack lasted, like the previous one, for about three quarters of an hour, until it got dark, and then they cleared off. During this attack nothing was hit, and I don't think any were brought down, but it was more unpleasant than the first one.

Lieutenant John Shaw, MC (RHG) is the final diarist and the second professional soldier. He came from Yorkshire farming stock and together with Valerian Douro was awarded the Military Cross for his valour in the capture of Palmyra in Syria. Prime Minister Churchill referred in the Commons to a 'ring of steel around Palmyra', but 1HCR's 'ring of steel' comprised Morris trucks and obsolete Hotchkiss machine guns, one from the museum in Hythe.

Captain Marquess Valerian Douro, MC (RHG) is older than the others. Born in Rome 'in a great hall frescoed with busts of Roman emperors' – hence his name Valerian – he is twenty-eight. Educated at Eton and

New College Oxford, where he joined the Bullingdon Club and was a close friend of Jack Profumo, Douro had left Oxford early, to his father's chagrin, to join up. Because of his name and pedigree and because he is a well seasoned. professional soldier, the younger officers, all volunteers, are rather in awe of him.

Lieutenant Henry, Earl of Uxbridge (RHG), A Squadron troop leader. Henry would inherit the title of Marquess of Anglesey and his ancestor also fought at Waterloo alongside the first Duke. He lost his leg, which prompted that famous exchange of plain speaking with the Duke: 'By God, sir, I've lost my leg!' 'By God, sir, so you have!'

His father saw action in the Regiment in 1914 and would never talk about it; but no such inhibition or reserve affects Henry. Uxbridge, when aged sixteen and a half, worked as a draughtsman technician, improving the ailerons on Lancaster Bombers. A buoyant, humorous man of great character, he has, even at that age, a flamboyant, artistic temperament. 'I rather enjoyed it all – and particularly enjoyed it when it went wrong – as I feel the Royal Family does now and again!' Later he is to write the monumental eight-volume *A History of the British Cavalry, 1816-1919*. But in contrast to many of the others, Uxbridge has, as he says, 'never been near a horse'.

Colonel Sir Robert Eric Sherlock Gooch, DSO (LG), Eleventh Baronet (Benacre Hall), Commanding Officer of 1HCR and paterfamilias of the Regiment, nicknamed 'Wispy' because of his luxuriant moustache, was, according to Uxbridge: 'oldish, which would mean about fifty!' He has been in the Regiment for 22 years, When he joined as a second lieutenant his servant was Trooper Hunt, who in 1943 was the only regimental figure with Great War service. Hunt is his 'solid block', as he is known, 'against wavering and adversity'.

Whenever possible Gooch insists on peacetime routine in the Officers' Mess, with members changing from battle to service dress, and the Orderly Officer announcing to the CO, 'Dinner is ready'. He had his own bath with him wherever he went and 'Hunt used to give him a good bath whenever they were sufficiently quiet.' Gooch is a universally admired central figure, leading from the front, sensitive and caring towards his men. In the Syrian campaign, for his organization of the advance on Palmyra, showing complete disregard for delays and danger, and calmness and sound judgment under at times very difficult conditions, he was awarded the DSO. Like all successful commanders he was concerned first and foremost for his men, and second with winning the battle. He exemplifies what General George Patton said on leadership during the Italian campaign: 'There has been a great deal of talk about loyalty from bottom to top. Loyalty from the top to the bottom is much more important, and also much less prevalent. It is this loyalty from the top to the bottom which binds juniors to their seniors with the strength of steel.'

Directly under Colonel Gooch is the Second in Command, Major Iain Merry, MC and Captain Ian Henderson, the Adjutant. There is an HQ Squadron, commanded by Major John Young, and three squadrons of 150 men each A, B, and C.

Major Tony Murray-Smith was A Squadron Leader, whose Second in Command is Valerian Douro, the only officer besides Gooch, Merry and Lieutenant John Shaw to be decorated. Douro has already been serving under Murray-Smith in Iraq, and so it is to continue: 'The great horseman …' They get on 'reasonably well. He had a fiery temper.' Du Plessis remembers him with less affection, someone 'never open to discussion', and that between him and Douro there was 'no love lost'. Van Ammel recalls Douro was a well seasoned, fearless soldier. 'When we are down on the Red Sea coast, he saw a snake; he got up and whacked it with his stick, eventually killing it.' Of Murray-Smith he says:

> Before Alamein he was in charge of Smith Force, a squadron of dummy A/Cs which had chassis of wood and canvas overlaid to make them look like Sherman tanks, and they moved by night so the deception could not be seen. Murray-Smith was a typical Midlands hunting man; to begin with as a young officer he had had a bad stammer and nearly gave up his commission, as he had so little confidence: as the war went on he became a commanding figure, so only a trace of the stutter remained.

CHAPTER THREE

CAIRO DAYS

The signs of poverty are very distressing: so many lives are devoted to the most inhuman tasks ... How depressingly ugly is the Egyptian of today! The veiled women are an unfortunate, unlovable lot. On badly balanced high-heeled shoes, they lope along sloppily, without looking where they are going, continuously colliding with one another or stepping under the wheels of the oncoming traffic.

Cecil Beaton, *Diaries 1941–44*

In the autumn of 1943 these young officers under their older professional superiors are assembled at Fayid Camp near Alexandria waiting to hear, as they expect, when they will be sent into Italy to engage the enemy.

The costly Allied invasion of Sicily on July 10, 1943, its failure – in so far as the German commander, Field Marshal Albert Kesselring, withdrew his main forces virtually intact to the Italian mainland – and the subsequent invasion of Italy with the landings at Salerno, the quick fall of Naples, followed by the slow and halting advance north, was of highly questionable value. Some with hindsight have commented that it was futile and ill-judged.

The consequences were that two and a half million men on both sides turned the whole of Italy into a bloody battlefield, with the population savagely brutalized by the Nazis, tens of thousands made prisoner, deported or murdered. Starvation, especially in the south and in Naples, took hold. The Nazis plundered land and industrial sources, while the military casualty lists weighed heavily against the so-called conquering Allied armies (approximately 2 if not 3 to 1), for all their bravery and dedication. The cost in blood for the combatants was enormous, but no less ravaged, starved and murdered were the people of Italy, its beautiful countryside and culture laid waste and often obliterated.

Fifteen days after the Sicily invasion Mussolini was forced to resign and was then arrested, while on September 3 Allied troops had landed on the Italian mainland at Salerno. As a consequence, Italy signed a secret armistice, followed by Marshal Badoglio's government declaring war on Germany. Badoglio had, since he resigned as Chief of Italy's armed services in 1940, passed the years playing cards and consuming champagne from his cellar. The pro-fascist King of Italy fled Rome, but in the confusing plots and counter-plots Field Marshal Albert Kesselring, the German commander, quickly made sure the Italian fleet and its 1.7 million troops, whose generals had fled, rapidly capitulated. 'I loved these people,' Kesselring said of the Italians. 'Now I can only hate them.'

Hitler ordered the Duce to be rescued from his imprisonment in a hotel in the Apennines. 'The Fuhrer now realises that Italy never was a power, is no power today and would not be a power in the future,' wrote Goebbels in his diary.

On September 12, 1943, the diarist Norman Lewis described the panic when American forces were almost wiped out by a Panzer division at Salerno:

> A line of American tanks went by, making for the battle, and hardly any time passed before they were back, but now there were fewer of them, and the wild and erratic manner in which they were driven suggested panic ... This afternoon distraught American ack-ack gunners brought down their third Spitfire. This had just flown from Sicily and taking off in pursuit of FW 190s was immediately shot down while flying at 300 feet.

German forces retreated from Salerno after a ten-day battle during which they almost pushed the tactically inept invading force back into the sea. Claiming victory in their ordered withdrawal, they scorched and salted the earth between Naples and Rome. No bridge or culvert was too small to escape the eye of the German demolition engineers.

After the bloody, costly battle to break out of the Salerno beachhead the Allies captured Naples and then, making the first of many subsequent blunders of military intelligence, they made the assumption that once Naples was lost, Hitler would abandon southern Italy. This was never to be the case.

So they found that far from speedy, the Allied advance, chronicled in Rick Atkinson's *Day Of Battle*, would be 'determined by bulldozers, if not by a nervous soldier on hands and knees probing for mines with a bayonet'. All roads led to Rome, the Allied Commander General Alexander joked, 'but all the roads are mined – as well as footpaths, lovers' lanes, alleys, goat trails, streambeds, shortcuts, and tracks, beaten and unbeaten.' At every opening for any advance the Germans put an obstacle. But the main obstacle was the mountainous terrain, which gave the defenders superiority.

Everything that was useful or could be eaten was taken, from able-bodied Italian men to horses and mares, through cattle, sheep (92%) and poultry (86%). Surplus saddles and horseshoe nails were torched, railroad tracks disabled. A dead German soldier's letter, found in his tunic, said, 'The Tommies will have to chew their way through us, and we will surely make hard chewing for them.'

So begins one of the biggest campaigns of attrition in the history of war, which sometimes approaches the scale of the First World War bloodbaths, or Hitler's invasion and defeat in Russia. It has never enjoyed the high profile and headlines these other battles have, even though, for example, the Salerno and Anzio bridges and beachheads were as dramatic in their promise as the Normandy landings in June 1944. As the eminent diarist Harold Nicolson recorded:

Wednesday September 15, 1943. I have recovered from my shattering disappointment over the Italian misfortunes. I had, I suppose, felt underneath that the surrender of Italy really meant the shortening of the war. I was angry and mortified that the Germans could exploit the situation so rapidly whereas we seemed to have lost every trick. But after four days of real distress, my old easy confidence has returned. I imagine that my feelings were typical of the mass of the people, although the ordinary citizen probably does not realise to the same extent as I do what a fillip the release of Mussolini will have given to German opinion. They will again feel themselves to be invincible.

Some argue that Marshal Badoglio's capitulation in the autumn of 1943 brought more disadvantages than advantages to the Allied cause. The battle-hardened *Landser* who confronted, with less than half the numbers, the hastily cobbled together American divisions and the more hardened Commonwealth divisions, extorted a prodigious price in blood and trial by combat. They were, although under-equipped and short of supplies, on the whole equal, if not better, soldiers.

One German officer at Salerno complained that though the enemy insisted on charging their Shermans right down the barrels of 88s and were picked off one after another, he 'ran out of ammunition before they ran out of tanks'. Kesselring believed the quality of most of the forces fighting him, by which he was outnumbered three to one, was little better than that of 'militias'.

By the end of 1943, before he is captured, escapes and then is recaptured, Mussolini has correctly judged that Hitler is losing the war and is distancing himself from further committing his army, navy and air force to support the Führer. Most Italians no longer support Hitler and have become vociferously anti-Axis. So if she had not changed sides, perhaps a virtually stagnant and feebly resistant Italy might have put up little fight against Allied pressure and brought the campaign to a close earlier.

By giving Hitler and his generals the excuse to activate Operation *Achse*, the *Wehrmacht* invasion of Italy, the luckless and strategically outmanoeuvred new Italian government (whose forces were not prepared sufficiently to confront German garrisons a tenth their size) robbed Allied leaders of the success of the fall of Rome, which would have buoyed up morale in their war-weary lands. In effect, Italy, by changing sides, brought materiel and manpower advantages to the Third Reich. Italian military equipment captured in 1943 assisted in rebuilding German units crippled in the various campaigns of 1944. The Swiss continued to aid Germany by keeping rail lines open through the Swiss Alps, citing their neutrality in rejecting the Allies' entreaties that they stop helping Hitler.

Military leadership without optimism is not possible, said Hitler in late 1943, replacing Rommel whom he had first appointed supreme commander in Italy, with Kesselring. 'I don't regard him as a stayer,' he said of Rommel, who later plotted against him. In November he decreed 'the end of withdrawals', and committed a million men to future defensive action at Cassino, Ortona, the Rapido River and Anzio.

As he did this, gloom descended on the Allied camp: the objective was Rome – but it was a long way off. The cost of what many saw as a needless campaign rose steeply in the autumn of 1943 and early months of 1944. It would entail a piling up of corpses on every front, gloved soldiers heaving Allied and Axis bodies onto the truck trailers, the living 'wrestling with the dead'.

The will of the Germans to continue the fight and add to the heaps of dead on the battlefield is summed up by Elias Cannetti in *Crowds and Power*:

> The fact wars can last so long, and may be carried on well after they have been lost, arises from the deep urge of the crowd to maintain itself in the acute stage; not to disintegrate ... This feeling is sometimes so strong that people prefer to perish together with open eyes, rather than acknowledge defeat and thus experience the disintegration of their own crowd.

An American veteran soldier, George Biddle, wrote, 'I wish the people at home, instead of thinking of their boys in terms of football stars, would think of them in terms of miners trapped underground or suffocating to death in a ten-strong fire. I wish they would think of them as cold, wet, hungry, homesick and frightened. I wish, when they think of them, they would be a little sick in their stomachs.'

***

Hindsight easily rearranges history to suit a theory. Lieutenant du Plessis, aged 19, on the ground at the time, points to the reality: 'There was an unwritten voice in the army, which never got out, that the army was a crazy establishment, which always got it wrong ... Officers were only informed what was going on, on a need-to-know basis, so, if you didn't need to know something you weren't told about it.' This was deliberate: 'It is wonderful how men can keep secrets they have not been told,' said Winston Churchill.

The 1st Household Cavalry Regiment knows little of what lies in store on the Italian mainland, although by now the men have a premonition that this will be their destination. Before they embark for Italy in spring 1944, to be deployed in the advance of the heavily defended spine of Italy, Colonel Gooch has to keep his Regiment occupied with manoeuvres and exercises, or mock battles, to prepare it. It has moved from Damascus in Syria through Tulkarm to arrive at El Fayid, a distance of more than 400 miles, on October 3, 1943. So the autumn months pass in maintenance, training, and exercises; at one time they transfer 50 miles to Sidi Bishr, at another for 'Exercise Bedouin', to the West Coast of the Bay of Suez.

On October 31, after the tenth divisional parade at Fayid, there is a march past, to the tune of 'Men of Harlech' played by the Royal Artillery band, and Major-General H. L .Berks DSO takes the salute. They drive, change camps frequently, mainly returning to Fayid, and are constantly on 24 hours notice to be sent into action.

They engage in skirmishes when the Vichy French seize the president and ministers of the Lebanese Republic and hold them prisoner in Rachaia Citadel, near Damascus. A force of Sherman tanks with C Squadron is sent to demand surrender, with the ultimatum that if this is withheld they will blow up the main gate of the Citadel. By then the main body of the Regiment is at Jabel Mazar. They drive to Merrjayoun, and finally 150 miles to Jerusalem, where a detachment mounts guard on King David Hotel. Second in command of this is Douro: Major St George is the CO, and it consists of two subalterns and 112 other ranks. Now quartered in a transit camp, they stay in Jerusalem nearly a week, and on December 2 the King David Hotel guard 'dismounts'.

Now they are on permanent standby leave for Italy, although such moves are often postponed. They have frequent range shooting practice with A/Cs, mortars, machine gun and small arms. Their battle readiness is enhanced by infrequent and highly unpopular 10- or 15-mile route marches – a foretaste of what is to come.

Before Italy the officers enjoy a lifestyle superior in some ways to that of bombed and rationed home. They train – not too much – they chase away the hours – they go shooting, carouse, place bets, pursue girls, write letters home, and while there are discomforts in being under canvas in the sand dunes, life maintains its momentum, as in pre-war days, of being, as du Plessis puts it, 'a nice easy house party'.

According to Ewart, du Plessis is 'always pursuing girls or causes' and with their man-servants they fare rather better, it seems, than their peers in England. Porchey misses his horses, true, about which he is constantly brought up-to-date from home. Rather greedily, and sometimes told off in the mess for eating too much, Porchey is the food barometer of the group, the gastronomic assessor. His letters detail quite sumptuous fare, especially at parties. Porchey's father writes to him about finding some salad oil to send home and he replies he will – and that's not all:

I will see what I can do about soap and stockings when I go to Cairo. Trousers corduroy, sweaters, shirts are always very useful. I don't know, but fancy you might get them coupon free. If you can't don't bother. Type of meals we get now – *Breakfast* Egg, Porridge, Eggs, Bacon, Sausages and Tea, Bread, Marmalade. *Lunch* Meat (tinned)/Spam, Rissoles, Salads, Potatoes (sweet or otherwise) Cauliflower or yellow Cabbage, Pears, Custard or Dried Apricots or Pineapple, Coffee, Cheese. Dinner, Soup, Meat and Sweet again usually hot fresh (camel!). As you see not too bad but always the same. Sweets one gets occasionally if someone goes to a town but there is the possibility of it being 150 miles away!

They all partake of these liberal breakfasts, and most smoke, although some officers are rigorous anti-nicotine enforcers. Van Ammel describes how one, Major Neil Foster ('Good solders aren't nice,' he says) 'was an absolute shit.' When he lit a cigarette after breakfast, 'there was this new officer in the mess [meaning Foster] and he came over and tore a strip off me. He could have come over and told me politely.' Captain Eion Merry, in spite of his name, spoke in monosyllables and was miserable; Major John Young was 'a very gentle fellow'.

Cairo may have held many and varied diversions for the young officers, but in the opinion of 58-year-old General George Patton, who since the invasion and capture of Sicily had become its Viceroy in Palermo, (where he read a biography of Douro's ancestor, the Iron Duke), it was a disgusting place. It looks, and the people act, Patton judged, like New York in 1928. Cecil Beaton, working as a war photographer, endorses this, but finds the colour and fragrance of the Casbah compensates for the squalor. Away from the fleshpots, Ewart gives a fair idea of the humdrum daily life at camp:

Monday, December 6. Reveille at 4.30 – Moved off at 6 – move across Sinai Desert. Went much faster and reached petrol point at about 3.30 – then went on to Fayid where we arrived at 7.30. One AEC had blow out so came in late. Bagged place in tent and off to bed early.

Tuesday, December 7. PT in morning – then maintenance – programme for the week – seems very busy. It is amazing how bad tempered everyone gets at Fayid. Settled into tent with Frankie [Williams], Porchey, Hall, Malby [Crofton] and Ned [The Hon E. Carson]. Paddy is on the outside. Rushed to get in first to ensure a place – it's so much more comfortable. Regimental mess again. Had lunch and dinner there. Rather worried about state of troop as [Trooper] Hope is now giving trouble as he wants to leave the Regiment and join the parachutists. Rumours that [Robin] Tudsbery, [Henry] Uxbridge, [Tony] Hall Bruce Coats and two others are over at Abbassia now. Had argument in evening with Herbert, Kenneth [Diacre] and Denis [Domvile], Porchey is definitely not getting on as well as he had hoped; beginning to see Kenneth and Herbert in true light – taking me some time.

Porchey is moved from A Squadron to C Squadron, but it seems he falls ill with a stomach bug. It is also at this time that he dates the Jerusalem Ambassador's daughter, called Priscilla; but this doesn't go too well. As he comments to his mother, 'She seems quite nice but like all the ladies in this part of the globe who have been here longer than six months, as tough as iron.' He also says Ewart is in good form, who on December 8 writes:

P.T. then maintenance and after that small kit inspection. Half following this afternoon. Slept, ate sweets and am just beginning to write letters. Just worked out how long we have been here, we found out 8 weeks since leaving England. Quite fantastic that in 5 weeks time almost completely settled down to this life which is different, and so different from what I have ever been? Herbert said a very true thing when he said 'There is no limit to human tolerance'. Must remember to write again in 4 months.

Ewart, more than most, maintains his devoted attachment to the Church:

Sunday, December 12. Got up at 6 to go to Mass at 7. Went to confession and communion. Padre gave me a lift back – seemed rather nice. Played rugger in Regimental trial – quite enjoyed game but was not picked for match in afternoon against RAF. When we returned I found eleven letters waiting for me from Home, June, Rupert and Celia. The home ones are by far the best – always the same. Celia is far too affectionate – June's was terribly welcome but Rupert's looked like it was written in rather a hurry.

In afternoon Ned Carson pulled my character to bits – very interesting in parts but not in others. He does not go half deep enough and as Malby says is rather superficial. Our extra kit is going to Abbassia so packed it today – it goes tomorrow early. Have just sat down before dinner to write letters and diary. It's going to be a busy evening. Managed to write very good careful letter home for Xmas. Tried to write to June [Kepple, daughter of Arnold Kepple] but was unsuccessful so will try again tomorrow.

The following Sunday Ewart is again at Mass:

Got up at 6.30 to go to Mass and communion at 7. After breakfast maintenance from 9–11. Conference about General Wilson's inspection on Wednesday. Played rugger for Service 1st and Service 2nd XV this afternoon. We were beaten. Quite disgraceful as they were terribly bad and we ought to have won. Porchey also played. After tea wrote to Celia being really blunt. Also home. G[avin Astor], Ned Carson came in late with Frankie [Williams] – pretended I was drunk so I got away with it. Threw stones instead of going to sleep.

On December 22 at 10 am the Regiment is inspected by Sir H. Maitland Wilson, the Commander-in-Chief of the Middle East, having bivouacked the night before in the parade area in the fork of the Ismailia-Suez Cairo roads. As in everything to do with the Regiment, the preparation and detail is meticulous: Included here are just two paragraphs of many to show the precision of their orders.

13. Each Sqn 2IC will carry one Yellow flag which he will pass to any vehicle which may break down. Any broken down vehicle will immediately hoist this yellow flag to indicate that he needs recovery. Any broken down vehicle will be passed by all following vehicles until it has been recovered. Should any vehicle break down, it will make no attempt to rejoin the Regiment until after the March Past.
14. The Salute. Marker flags will be 20 yds before the Saluting Base and 20 yds after the Saluting Base. Guns will be dipped at the first marker and remain dipped until the second marker. Officers only will stand to attention in the turrets and salute. Our Comdrs only will stand to attention in turrets, remain 'Eyes Front' and NOT salute. Officers in vehicles with sliding roofs will salute standing with their head shoulders out through

the roof. O.R's whether sitting in cabs or in the backs of vehicles will sit to attention 'Eyes Front' with rifles perpendicular between their knees. Officers differently counted will sit to attention and 'salute'.
W.O. Diary 17 Dec 43

And so we come to Christmas Day, 1943. In the Italian campaign to capture Rome, Major-General John Lucas noted that Fifth Army had 23,000 hospital admissions, and that 'we will get weaker instead of strong ... because I figure this is becoming a secondary theatre'. The Germans were satisfied that the Allied advance was 'equal to six miles per month'. Ewart:

Went to Mass and communion at 10am – then watched Senior Officers v Senior NCOs football match. Attended mess lunch when Colonel [Gooch] made rather clever speech. Chamberlain called me over to talk – thought that there would be trouble but I laughed heartily and managed to avoid it. Went to sleep in afternoon. Had excellent dinner with quite a lot to drink. After dinner went to the NCO's mess and I don't know what I drank but it made me really quite drunk. I was absolutely clear in my head but I know I had too much. Trouble with Paddy! Practically all the C's of H [Corporals of Horse = Sergeants] were drunk. Tony was. Squadron Leaders were all very funny and amusing. I wonder whether it has good or bad effect.

After Christmas out of the 1HCR base in Fayid they began manoeuvres; the Regiment, part of the 10th Armoured Division, now consists of thirty-nine officers commanded by Gooch. The total strength varies between 525 and 550, which is to be increased when a fourth (D) Squadron is added later. They are equipped with approximately 180 vehicles: the A/Cs, being Daimlers, White Scout cars or half-tracks for carrying infantry, Dingos, which were Daimler two-man scout cars, and larger American Staghounds for Squadron and Regimental HQs.

At the end of December, again back in the desert at Fayid, they engage in prolonged manoeuvres and simulated battles ('Exercise Figpicker'), during which one Corporal and two troopers are accidentally wounded by a hand grenade. During these three months only one soldier has died, from malaria. After further exercises of simulated battle conditions ('Exercise Tussle'), 'mounted again', they move in the New Year from Fayid camp by train and on foot to Sidi Bishr, where by mid-February their trucks, new Staghounds, and Daimler Scout cars and A/Cs join them. 'Tussle' is described in the War Office Diary:

> The Germans were advancing from the Sudan. The Regiment would advance south covering the Corps front, contact enemy, and report on the strength of the enemy main body.
>
> 2130 C.O. issued orders. C Sqn to move out at 2300 hrs to Cairo, then move South down the Nile as far as El Burumbul thence East to Zafarama. The remainder of the Regiment with A Sqn leading to move out at 0330 hrs 28 Dec., and advance down the coast ...
>
> ... 30. 0930. The C.O. received orders from Major General H.L. Birks, DSO. The enemy was advancing in force on Ras Gharib. H.C.R. to cover the Corps front and delay the enemy until the evening of 1 Jan 1944., when the Corps would be concentrated Ain Sukana. No support is available until evening of 1 Jan 44.
>
> 1130. C.O. issued orders. C Sqn to take up a line of observation 64 Northing with one Troop on West flank, both with the task of delaying and harassing the enemy as much as possible. B Sqn to take up a defensive position in the Wadi Abu Khaleifi. A Sqn in reserve and to recce a position at Pt. 20 ....
>
> ... 31 0330. Enemy reported advancing North. C Sqn withdraw fighting delaying actions. The one Troop on the West flank caused considerable embarrassment to the enemy by shooting up transport and supplies.
>
> 1330. C Sqn withdraw through B Sqn. B Sqn attacked by tanks and had to withdraw. In the meantime A Sqn took up a position at Pt. 206, through which B Sqn withdrew. A Sqn held this position until dawn 1 Jan 44. Cpl. Forman, Tprs Andrew and Bull were accidentally wounded during the night by a hand grenade.

Ewart takes up the account of 'Figpicker' in detail at his own more personal level:

Monday, December 27. Written 6 days late. Prepared all morning for leaving Fayid by tonight. Quite a job getting everything organized as 6th troop scout car has now come to me temporarily and I have now got nowhere to put things. Left most of them on my Humber – I think this causes some discomfort ... No mess trunk to put suit cases on as there is no room in it so had to wangle it on to spare crews' lorry. In evening Major-General Birks commanding 10th Armoured Division came to dinner and afterwards gave out his orders to the Colonel. C Squadron left that night to go down the Red Sea route via Cairo. We slept by our cars with Reveille next morning at 2.30am, for exercise 'Figpicker'.

Tuesday, December 28. Reveille was at 2.30 and left at 4 from Fayid to reach the start line of the Cairo-Suez Rd at 6am. We actually reached it at 5am. Teddy Lambton was leading with 4th Troop, then me and then the Squadron leader. We advanced by Suez and then straight along by the Red Sea past the FA Post and Suchaa. On the way we met several small parties of enemy and different Troops took the lead the whole time. Finally when we had advanced 20 miles Tony himself was 'killed'. By this time Teddy, Bert Carter with No 1 Troop, Ian Van Ammel with No 2 been in the lead and had been ½ or entirely wiped out. B squadron was then sent through to take up the lead and we followed in the rear. We advanced peacefully all day and leaguered just North of the Zafarama light house ...

... *Wednesday, December 29.* Reveille at 6.00 – we then dispersed and moved off at 6.30 just about 2 miles to the Zafarama light house. Here we had breakfast and luckily got some water from the wog garrison – we were rationed for the scheme to ½ gallon a day. Also some sugar. We stayed here for some hours whilst B squadron was slightly ahead of us. Eventually C Squadron came down the pass behind us and passed through us. That evening Figpicker was said to have ended and we drove on about 45 miles to reach some oil wells. Here we harboured the night.

Thursday, December 30. This morning we had a rest from the exercise – maintenance all morning. Divisional Commander had conference with all officers this morning. He seemed to be very sound and know his job. Had my face dressed again – this time with bandages – It really has been the most terrible nuisance. We left at 2pm for W. El Deir, about 45 miles away. We were now on the Retreat. C Squadron was out in front in points of observation – B Sqn was holding a position about 10 miles back and we were behind RHQ in reserve. Spend a very peaceful night.

Friday, December 31. In the morning we recce'd position behind us but before we could recce 2nd position thoroughly we heard over the wireless that B Squadron were being pressed forward. We therefore rushed back and got into the 1st position which was under Valerian and consisted of No's 3 in front then No's 2, 4 and 5 Troops ... The 1st position did not last long so we had to withdraw. When we arrived at the 2nd position the Colonel was there and as I had not recce'd it properly took some time getting into it whilst Tanks were moving on. ...

Could not find line of withdrawal with Cpl Worth's AEC – he flapped like anything – I don't think he would be much good in action. Eventually after great trouble and many hectic moments, got in position. When darkness fell Bongos began to attack and we withdrew. Tony stayed with 2, 4 and 6 Troops.

Captain Mantel, an English speaking Pole in the Carpathian Lancers, part of General Anders' Polish Corps, had accompanied the Regiment on 'Figpicker', which he calls 'a scheme'. On his way there Mantel, who was adjutant, was accompanied by his second-in-command and his LAD [Light Aid Detachment] officer. 'On the way we passed many camps with their camouflaged tents until we finally spotted the stables through our binoculars where the armoured cars stood in lines with their gaily coloured pennants fixed to their aerials.'

They have tea in the officers' mess, and here meet Gooch, Merry and Henderson. They find everything impressive, admiring Gooch's handling of his men, and are in awe of his grasp of detail. After tea they stroll round the camp, where there are fires all round in the darkness and the 'lancers', as Mantel calls them, are brewing their last mugs of tea before bedding down. Next morning, two hours before dawn, when the 'lancers' are packing up to move off, it is bitterly cold – they had brought their long white sheepskins and many of the officers were similarly clad. A hot substantial breakfast follows – everything works so smoothly. The L.A.D. officer watches the recovery teams going into action and marvels at the speed they rescue armoured vehicles bogged down in soft patches of mud or sand.

***

51

January passes with rumour and counter-rumour. Now most believe the war is almost over, and that they will never see action beyond the complicated and costly mock battles. Some are growing up fast, others are not.

On January 21 Ewart reports he gets a rocket for going too close to enemy positions on a 'scheme', and that he has been 'unreliable, must try and improve'. Next day he is absent from his troop to have his finger dressed for a desert sore and gets another dressing down. There are issues with swearing: on the order to parade at reveille Cpl Hills says 'bollocks' and Cpl Worth 'then said he would take him before the Sqn Leader. He went up and is being sent before the Colonel. I went to Mass, confession and communion and whilst I was away apparently Tony got all officers and Cpl Majors together and said that discipline was getting slack and that any answering back must be dealt with immediately.' Once again he is told off for wearing a sheepskin coat by Ian Henderson, the Adjutant.

Meanwhile, Valerian has left for Jerusalem to get married. Ewart reports on January 26, two days before the wedding, 'Tony Murray-Smith, Colonel's second-in-command, Guy Routledge, Ian Henderson and Gerard Leigh, all go to Valerian's wedding to daughter of the Governor of Palestine [Major-General Douglas McConnel].'

Diana McConnel and Valerian met only at the end of November in 1943 in the King David Hotel, and after a short but intense few weeks of burgeoning love were hesitating over whether or not to marry. Jerusalem was almost the perfect setting for wartime romance to come quickly to a head. Hermione, the Countess of Ranfurl, as quoted by Valerian's daughter in her book, *A Journey through my Family*, records:

> To drive along the streets of Jerusalem is never boring – one sees Jewish men in flat, fur-edged hats with their uncut hair falling over their shoulders; Arab women in tall, almost medieval headdresses; Greek priests with buns and stove-pipe hats; officers of the Transjordan Frontier Force with high black fur headgear slashed with scarlet to match their belts; Arab Legion, Abyssinian clergy, Palestine Police, Americans, Bedouin, and British uniforms – it is quite a fashion show.

To add spice the city was racked with danger and suspicion. Diana worked in Jerusalem as her father's ADC, and she and Valerian met when he was stationed guarding the hotel during the visit of VIPs. Of Jerusalem's complications, Diana said, 'Wherever you go there is an unspoken mental undertow of suspicion. No one asks but everyone wants to find out which side you are on – Arab or Jew.' Jane Wellesley writes:

> In December 1943 Valerian Douro was a handsome twenty-eight-year-old who had overcome a difficult childhood to emerge as a self-confident young man who wanted to enjoy life to the full. Eton had given him freedom from the complications of home life; Oxford, an education; the army, security and lasting friendships; and war had challenged him with responsibility and commitments. He was upper-class, but with a twist of Bohemia through the intellectual, artistic and separated lives of his parents. He was glamorous and eligible, and had a string of girlfriends behind him, some, like the Druze Princess Amal al-Atrash, with colourful reputations. Finally, through a tragic act of war, he had become the heir to a famous dukedom. He was not a straightforward catch.
>
> At twenty-one Diana Ruth McConnel was a lustrous beauty, five foot six, with a mass of dark hair, huge green eyes, a fantastic figure and a warm, dimply smile. Her Scottish background celebrated industry, enterprise and an adherence to strict religious morality. She was a precious only child – all the more so because her birth sealed the impossibility of her parents having any more children.

The couple dine by candlelight in the roof garden restaurant and cabaret. The courtship proceeds to engagement and he gives her a ring with a huge cabochon emerald set in diamonds. Valerian asks his prospective father-in-law for his daughter's hand. 'Are you a salmon fisherman?' Douglas asked his future son-in-law, only half in jest. Valerian, hands behind his back with fingers crossed, replied immediately, 'Certainly, General!'

They, and everyone else, were worried about what might happen to Valerian when he went again into action. As His Grace (who is Eighth Duke) told me, 'So I left the decision to her whether we should get married before we went to Italy, or afterwards, and in January we got married.'

Some days before the January 28 wedding Diana discovers in her office an intelligence document warning of a murderous plot by the Jewish terrorist Stern Gang, dedicated to ousting the British from Palestine. The plot is to plant a bomb in St George's Cathedral, where they are to marry, targeted to kill the high-ranking wedding guests – the High

Commissioner, Chief of Police, Chief Judge, Colonel Glubb Pasha and Diana's father.

John Ewart's 20th birthday falls on the Thursday before the wedding:

> Rugger practice then maintenance all morning. Clean guns. Got cable from home – letter from Mr Monk and lot of parcels. In afternoon small kit inspection. In evening had party at Officers Club – consisted of Porchey, Frankie Williams, Laurence Rook, Herbert du Plessis, Paddy B-Bruce, Ned Carson, Dennis Domvile, Kenneth Diacre and Ian Van Ammel. We really had a most excellent dinner with a private room to ourselves – everybody drank too much. I didn't really think that it was a tremendous success – although people said that they enjoyed themselves. COH Dooley came to pick us up – so we bought him in for a drink.
>
> It's funny I can't believe I am only just 20 and have been leading a troop of 14 men. Oh how proud I feel of myself – absolutely no right to. But I do.

Porchey describes the same event in a letter to his father, Lord Carnarvon, whom he addresses as 'Darling Pups':

> We went out last night to the local club for John Ewart's birthday party ... Very good dinner – Crab Soup/Fried and Fish/Roast and/Jellys/Canapé, Canard, Coffee, Champagne (Syrian type) Liqueurs. Very good. Really. Teddy Lambton is very funny about you, makes me roar with laughter, also talking racing in general. I amused a lot of them ... by mimicking as best I could the people they asked me to – Dick Dawson, Harry Cottrill, Harry Rosebery, Fred Cripps and the Aga Khan, Lord Sefton, Tommy McDougall, Lord Beaverbrook, Lady Muse, Michael Beary. I tried hard to remember all your odd movements and conversation and they liked the Aga talking to Dick Dawson best ...

On the night of Ewart's birthday in Jerusalem they discover the bomb planted in an arch on the approach to the Cathedral door and remove it, foiling the plot. There is no terror or panic in either bride or groom.

In winter sunshine the official car carrying Douglas and his daughter sweeps through that arch to arrive at St George's Cathedral. Dressed in heavy white silk and carrying white orchids, tied with an olive green ribbon, the bride looks ravishing.

Everyone kneels for the final patriotic hymn, 'O Perfect Love' with its line, 'I vow to thee my country' as the couple leave, saluted by raised swords of the Mounted Police guard of honour, ex-soldiers from the Blues.

The honeymoon in Beirut quickly comes to an end because Douro is put on stand-by for departure to Italy. Almost at once the Regiment moved to Alexandria. The couple manage to stay at Shepheard's Hotel in Cairo when Diana visits, and 'they had to run the gauntlet of a bar filled with friends every evening. Hot chocolate at Gropis was a more calming ritual.'

Valerian's call still had not come but Diana's leave had run out and she returned to her desk at Jerusalem HQ to resume her duties. 'I worried about marrying Diana and then having to go off.'

Ewart is by now making assessments of character. The first is on his A Squadron Leader Tony Murray-Smith:

Tony quite a fine character – strong – jumps out of bed for PT in the morning – shouts for any little reason – does not let anybody get away with anything – quite wonderful for he keeps people up to scratch – and all this week he is obviously just as tempted by human feelings as anyone. Never seeks popularity – is not too proud to learn – at one time I got the impression he thought very deeply on everything – changed mind in a way as I think he is naturally very good. I wonder what he would be like not in the army? No friends? Has he any religious feelings?

In spite of John's desire to know him better the Squadron Leader keeps his distance, so nothing much changes in John's view, or as he elliptically puts it, 'Not changed much, feel that best way is to take as fact that I will never get on really well with him and therefore avoid on parade.' He goes on weighing up the characters:

Kenneth Diacre [he later marries Ian Van Ammel's sister]. One of the few interesting characters in the Regiment – have not yet really fathomed it yet – deep – but not deep enough to be sensible about religion – or is it because he cannot control his emotions and does not want to be a hypocrite? He suffers because he has been spoilt although he does not think this. If he had had some brothers he would have learnt more give and take. Has the art of flattering one when it pleases him and this helps him get away with things. Although he is obviously clever, he does not know as much as he should about History etc – likes to make out he does and fully believes that we are all taken in by his apparent knowledge. Want to give him this but he undoubtedly is very shallow, so it isn't worth my time.

Time drags during the next three months, and it becomes the same round of inspections, gunnery practice, squash, bridge, regimental parties, expectations rapidly dashed of meeting girls. 'It seems our moving has been put off again,' John notes on 15 March 1944. 'I often wonder if we will ever fight.'

***

It is hardly a surprise that the longer any body of soldiers remains in any one place the greater the attachment grows to local people, especially young and unattached women. Between extended exercises in the desert around the camp at Fayid, forays into the neighbouring territories to put down rebellion or bolster British rule, the young officers drive off to Cairo or Alexandria, play bridge, find partners to dance with, and most of all – little surprise here – get drunk.

Some officers form relationships with local women, Herbert du Plessis, Ian Henderson and Ian Van Ammel do, which causes problems. 'Twenty-eight investigations of prospective brides for servicemen complete to date, of which twenty-two proved to be prostitutes,' writes Norman Lewis, an Intelligence Corps NCO charged with investigating such cases. 'COs must realise that everything possible will be done to discourage such marriages.'

Fraternisation and entanglement with girls is scrutinised very carefully by Colonel Gooch. Ian Henderson becomes engaged and they have a party to celebrate. The adjutant, whom everyone likes, is also smitten. 'He and I had fallen in love with two Jewish sisters,' du Plessis remembers:

> She was a lovely Jewish girl called Colette. The Jews of Cairo were highly respected people, they were the financiers and Ian Henderson was deeply, deeply committed to the elder sister of this girl. The Colonel was desperate about it because he did not want Ian to commit himself to marry some girl in Cairo just before he was due to go back to England, and then contract what he thought was a proper marriage. There he saw me following in the same footsteps, so he locked us in.

The incarceration or 'gating' of Herbert comes about in a slightly unconventional manner:

> I expect there are some bits about me in not very good colour! [He is recalling this in company with Van Ammel and the author.] Do you remember, Ian, when we were in Alexandria waiting to go to Italy? I was the duty officer one night with order to turn out the guard at 10 o'clock, then 3.30. I failed on my duty at 3.30, and it was that night a robbers' raiding party broke in and went off with newly delivered long range binoculars. They must have seen what was going on and they struck.
>
> Next morning there was consternation around the breakfast table, and I arrived and said, 'What's the problem?' They said 'the binoculars have been stolen and what time did you turn out the guard?' I said, 'Never mind that.' But I had to go and report to Ian. I said, 'Ian I am sorry but I can't report what happened at 3.30 because I did not indeed turnout the detail.'
>
> I was taken to Wispy. But he was delighted because he was trying to keep me out of the close involvement with the lady in Cairo. 'This is my chance to lock up Herbert so he can't get into problems. Right, Herbert, you're gated for 8 days' – long enough – so I wasn't able to go and see the love of my life at the time, or say goodbye, or even pick up the photo we had done by a professional.

Another roistering young officer is Captain de Piava Raposa, the LAD officer. 'Tony Murray Smith in a stroke of brilliance christened him Pavlova. He was tall, darkish, suntanned, an elegant man you could well imagine in tights dancing. Fell in love with a girl in Cairo, Milly, and she got married to the REME officer.'

'One night Piava Raposo,' says Van Ammel, taking up the story, 'came back from Cairo and said, "I have just met the finest f*** in Cairo" – it was a little bit extreme ... But in fact he did marry that girl in Cairo and was very happy.'

Van Ammel, too, has a girlfriend in Beirut, a White Russian princess. He shows me her photograph. Others, like Ewart, are more circumspect about the local beauties:

> It seems that I must either have Religion with all its implications or a woman who amuses me. I'm just beginning to understand the value of marriage. Like all other things it's almost unbelievable that one did not

know it before. Dinner at Union Club after joining Union Club and having a bath. Six of us were going to *Merry Widow* but when we arrived to dine 7 people were there. Muddle with Paddy [Brudenell-Bruce]. I was furious. Everyone was dining in the same place. Eventually I managed to get to opera with great difficulty. Got back rather late. Cairo depresses me no end – the smell and the terrible people – they live in such filth. I was just feeling really depressed when I met Malcolm and Laurence [Rook] just arrived. Laurence fixed up a party with FANY [First Aid Nursing Yeomanry] and it was in great spirits that I went to D.P.O. and posted parcels to home 3 girls ... and Celia. Then changed and we went off to fetch the girls – unfortunately we could not raise any other girls so I dined with Malcolm at the Club du Turf.

John, aged 87, in a similar way to Ian, confides in me about his thoughts of those times:

Those days relationships with girlfriends were absolutely different from today. Celia [Anson, John's girlfriend] wrote lots and lots of letters to me, every day, I wrote a few. She was never commissioned, she always served in the ranks, sent up to the North of Scotland as a WREN. She loathed every moment of it. I kept well clear of girlfriends in any case, if they,(the others, had girlfriends they probably got some disease, and I always thought I'm not interested in any of that, I was just out of school.

Generally they steer away from fellow nationals, unless they are new arrivals for, as mentioned earlier, Porchey considered that 'women over six months out were tough'.

Shepheard's Hotel is the recreational auberge. On Saturday February 5, Ewart is there:

In morning Tony came back – handed over cars to 27th C and went away for leave about 11 am. Ian Van Ammel managed to get extra and we both hitched using different methods but we all arrived with John Shaw at Shepheards Hotel at the same time. Managed to get into a room with a Major Flower, R.B. who was very quiet and hardly said a word. Had dinner with Ian at L'Auberge De Turf – in evening went to low Café called Badin. Some almost fantastic displays by horrible women. Went to Georgian Club and saw racing. Reminded me slightly of England.

Porchester, to all intents and purposes, maintains his traditional life style. As befits a future Racing Manager to the Queen and a Founder Chairman of the Game Research Association he keeps up with the stable news from Highclere and the latest gossip in *Sporting Life*, as well as organising regimental boxing matches.

Cairo is only a few hours away, so there is a lot of fun and distractions to be had: films (*Casablanca*, *The Phantom of the Opera*), operas, books, girls and clubs – and not least, for the hunting and shooting core of the Regiment, plenty of game. Fraser:

Saturday February 26. Got up at 4.30 am, had breakfast and left Shepheards at 5.30 am for British Embassy. Left there in car at 6.0am arrive. Ekiad Shoot at 8.30 am. Met H.E. on the way. 17 guns in all. Shot all morning, wonderful fun, never seen so many duck or snipe about before. Total bag 733. I got 6 duck and 2 snipe. Back in Cairo by 5.30 pm. Went to bed early as was very tired.

An undated letter of Porchey's expands on Fraser's entry. There are discrepancies – whose body count is one to believe?

I went for the weekend to Cairo stayed at Shepheards Fri night, dined there and saw Peter Stanley, who has been in 3 or 4 regts, and has a girl in tow. On Sat morning early we left for the embassy (5.45am) and then went in convoy 18 guns to the shoot at Lake Ekiad. The guns were HE (British Ambassador Lord Killearn) AOC Norman Smith, a South African, Sir (Alexander) Kewon-Boyd (director, ministry of the interior, Cairo), Dr Harting, Lord Cadogan MC, Peter Playdell-Bouverie, Maj Dick Marsh, a friend of Lord Dudley's in his car. I went with Eion Merry our second-in-command, Prince Galitzine, Laurence Rook, Malcolm Fraser, Giles Bay, I forget the others. We arrived, were dished out with 200 cartridges a piece and then we started off to our butts ... After HE had fired the first shot we started. I shot fairly well seeing it was with 'Lucan's' (H C Armstrong, author of *Grey Wolf* and *Lord of Arabia*) gun no 4 shot no ejectors. I shot 28 teal and 26 shoveller mallard, 1 pochard, 1 snipe (57) and fired 190 cartridges. I shot for three-quarter hour non-stop and then Finis. Total bag was 760 duck, 2 snipe, HE shot with 6 shot and 3 12 bores and killed, from the best butt I'm told, 136 duck picked up. ... We then returned to the Auberge du Turf for dinner and went to bed.

CHAPTER FOUR

SETTING SAIL FOR NAPLES

I have seen the great vision of Italy raising itself from the muck in which the Germans keep it mired.

Stendhal, *The Charterhouse of Parma*

The Regiment's removal from Camp Fayid is imminent. Daily its men are ordered to be prepared to move, only to have the order rescinded – but to where? Garrison duty, the south of France, to England for the planned invasion later in the year, to the Balkans?

Armoured reconnaissance units, such as 1HCR, are constantly at the forward extremes of the main battle areas, where they are screening and probing. Like high-maintenance horses used for hunting or competition where skill, speed and flexibility is paramount, they are rarely left to slog out a battle, or to eliminate a major force. They are pulled out of big battles, leaving them to artillery, tanks and infantry, and are sent elsewhere or further on to pursue or probe. When the enemy is losing or in retreat, their skills are most valuable, because they can assess enemy movement, essential for planning an advance.

Ideally, the officers of such units need forensic skills in understanding the kinaesthetics of battle: and for this, they have to be individuals. They tend to have moral codes, a sense of honour, a fairness in their approach both to their men and themselves, because if you are relying on judgment, understanding and perception in battle, you need *amour-propre*, a self-esteem in order to make the sacrifice of exposing yourself and those under your command to enemy fire, which sometimes you are not in a position to, or asked not to, return.

They are not primarily killers, and body counts or prisoner numbers do not appear prominently in their Regiment or personal diaries. Exposed constantly as they are to death, to capture, to the mechanical and communications breakdown of their 'mounts', they need the best equipment. They need to be continually mobile and adaptable, and to remedy set-backs and breakdowns with speed.

In 1943 the mindset of officers and men remains aristocratic, still underpinned as it has traditionally been by the hierarchy of class and land ownership. De Toqueville defined the essence of a stable aristocracy as having land as its basis, 'which clings to the soil that supports it; for it is not by privileges alone, nor by birth but by landed property handed down from generation to generation that aristocracy is constituted. A nation may present immense wealth and extreme wretchedness; but unless those fortunes are territorial, there is not true aristocracy, but simply the rich and the poor.'

Now, in February, they catch the train from Fayid to Sidi Bishr, a journey of over ten hours. Sidi Bishr is just outside Alexandria and three-quarters of a mile from the sea. 'Nice clean sand, but tents are smaller and more squashed. Train best way of getting into Alex. Lots of shooting to be had.' (Fraser.)

Four three-ton trucks, four fifteen-hundredweight trucks, twelve Daimler armoured cars, twelve Daimler scout cars, plus three Staghounds are collected by ninety other ranks from Abbassia. Range practice, tactics lectures, Brens and mortar practice intensify. 'It looks like things are beginning to move,' reports Ewart.

In the heated preparations more accidents occur: on March 4 two senior NCOs, RQMC (Regimental Quartermaster Corporal Major) Roebuck and SCM (Sergeant Corporal Major) Pout are seriously injured when they fall out of a lorry. Roebuck survives, but two days later when Ewart is duty officer:

> Woke up about 6.10 and found that clock had stopped and that I had not turned out guard. Went over to guard tent and found out there had been no trouble during the night. Will not make guard report unless asked for. Went on dull parade and Tony came along and said that poor old Corporal Major Henry Pout died last night – a bit shattering as he was so well a few

days ago – Everyone takes the news calmly as it is forgotten after almost an hour. It's funny what a system the army has. No man will ever stop things going. [But there is a big turnout for the funeral next day.]

This leads to John becoming introspective.

I can still see how unformed my character is – I am terribly influenced by other people – I don't know whether I want to be a J [Jesuit], to marry early and disappear to China [where his father has a business] – to wait at home and learn the business from that point of view. I would love to have a house in Leicestershire or Warwickshire.

Later in March the CO acquires a further fifteen Staghounds, eight Daimler Attack cars, twelve Daimler scout cars, eight three-ton lorries, eight fifteen-hundredweight trucks and four jeeps, which surely demonstrates how under-equipped the regiment has been in its training and mock battles. At the same time, the squadrons are sent on route marches without their vehicles. At the end of March Gooch arrives with 'encouraging news for our early move'. A terrific hurricane blows up, with the worst sandstorm Egypt has had for many years, tents are blown down everywhere. The Officers' Mess tent is torn to shreds, and blinding sand hampers exercises and maintenance. Next day there is still a strong wind. On March 31 Ewart tells his diary:

For the last two or three days, rumours have been spreading that we are to move shortly, and this afternoon at 1600 hrs the Col. spoke to the whole regiment outside the orderly room at Sidi Bishr. We are to go overseas very shortly, destination officially unknown, but most of us know it is Italy.

They 'hand in' their cars and prepare to move.

April 1. Cars went in this morning. Went to Alex with Porchey in afternoon – cashed cheque for £25. Went to cinema. Then dined with Domski [Revertera] and Porchey. It just seems to be coming clearer that in the near future we might be facing death. I am completely terrified of going into action but somehow I should imagine less terrified than most people. I think that I would do my job not because of bravery but because I would be terrified of what people think of me if I did not. I must strive for that very shallow reason – but try and bring my religion far closer to me and do it as the will of God. If only I could get back that spirit when everything is done cheerfully, as God's will, I would be a happy man.

Virtually all the officers are Anglicans or Roman Catholics, the latter including du Plessis and Revertera. The former attend services conducted by the Reverend P.L. Richards, the padre. The Sunday before they embark for Italy, Ewart is at Mass and benediction as usual – then to the Union Club in Alexandria with du Plessis and Fraser. He reads Plato and Cicero and on arrival back at camp argues with Herbert 'on the Russian question'. He spends two hours before he goes to bed writing to Celia by paraffin lamp.

Fraser, just to show how serious these young officers are, has been reading *Into Battle* by Churchill, and nursing a swollen, infected hand which has been causing him excruciating pain. This only gradually clears up – no antibiotics in those days. He can't go on the assault courses, but recovers by mid-March. April 3: 'Regiment leaves Sidi Bishr at 1900 hrs. March to Station. All night train journey to Port Said – not too bad as we were only 4 in our compartment. We arrived at Port Said about 9 am about 4 hours late!'

The Regiment then 'marches' from Port Said to cross the Suez Canal and spends the night 'in a transit camp just by the docks. A horrible place but we had our beds and a tent luckily. Next day the Regiment marches to the quay.'

Fraser has been rehearsing for an Easter Passion play at camp but has to leave that behind, along with the Egyptian money that they change for the British military equivalent. They catch a lighter to a P&O liner, SS *Strathnaver*, which is, as Ewart says, 'nice inside'. Ewart and Fraser share a cabin and play a lot of bridge with John still losing. They remain in port over Good Friday and John regrets he cannot go to Holy Communion every day. 'The food on the ship was very good but we had over 6,000 troops on board, mostly Poles and a few Cypriots. There were three sittings for meals – ours was the 3rd so we had breakfast at 0930hrs, lunch at 1400 hrs and dinner at 2000 hrs.' If the ship sank, comments Ewart, 'no organisation could cope with the muddle.' Some officers are not too happy to be on a dry ship. Van Ammel told me:

By now ships in convoy at sea were 'dry' – since the Americans entered the war. A very senior warrant officer coming on board, when he got to the staircase, just about to disappear into the bowels of the *Strathnaver*, dropped his carefully hidden bottle of whisky. You could see it plummeting slowly down – met by a gale of laughter from the heroic British. They were going off to get themselves killed – yet they could laugh! A moment to savour!

Ewart, on April 7:

Good Friday. I remember about 2 months ago Frank Williams told me that in time I would have complete control of my troop and feel that is happening more and more. Sometimes I find it far harder to work with men not in troop. Bridge all morning and part afternoon. Still losing. Begin writing first letter, had bad back.

Then at last they sail!

We turned around at about 0630 hrs on the 8th and proceeded down the harbour and out into the open sea. The whole journey by sea could not have been calmer and although it blew a bit one day, we barely pitched at all. Convoy: 12 ships. Everything went quite normally all the way, so I will continue from approximately 1700 hrs on 11th April '44. At about this time, we found ourselves approaching the Straits of Messina. Sicily was on our left and you could see the 'toe' of Italy, quite plainly on our starboard side, looking lovely in the setting sun. As we passed Mount Etna the sun went down behind it and it was silhouetted most beautifully. Mount Etna is 10,600 ft and with binoculars it was quite easy to see snow on the tips. Then it quickly got dark, which was a pity as we had no chance to see the Straits as we went through.

We passed through the Straits at about 9pm. They are about 5 miles across and there were lights on both sides, and the mountains were just visible as dark masses on either side of us. The lights on our right were doubtless Reggio – I wished so much that I had been able to see it all in daylight.

John Shaw is especially delighted to share a cabin on the top deck, near the boats, and compliments the catering, relishing a 'damn good kipper' served on Good Friday, the first he's seen for three or four years.

Porchey, expansive as ever in his correspondence, demands racing news constantly from 'Darling Pups' – Lord Carnarvon – and the stable staff at Highclere; but with an eye to censorship he hardly mentions the crossing to Italy. He draws one comparison to the earlier voyage from England. 'This time I was not at all seasick and won a £5 at bridge which we played continually' (most of this probably from John). Ewart:

> *April 10.* Played bridge and read all day. Our table is a very funny one – so many conflicting personalities. Kenneth [Diacre] always wanting his own way, and holding the limelight by his rather bubbly personality which he flogs to get more out of it. Ned [son of the famous Ulster separatist Carson, known from his low brows as Neanderthal Ned] very funny at times but rather overcome between Kenneth and Happy [Younghusband] – always wants to be talking or sulking ... Herbert – vague – sincere not really caring? Porchey looking at Kenneth – Frank [Williams] nice to everyone and insignificant and gradually seeing people in their true light.

Fraser rises to appreciate the scenic grandeur on April 12 but also sights destruction:

> We woke up today to find the ship passing close between Capri and the Italian mountains, all the way up they are simply enormous. No wonder the going had been so slow. There were clouds on the tops but with glasses it was not difficult to see several houses gutted and a lot of pill boxes in prominent positions. There was one big building right on the top of one mountain which must have been a German stronghold I should think. Then at about 10.00am we passed a very large convoy of merchantmen going south. About 40 ships all empty, with an escort of 4 destroyers. The mist by this time was covering most of the slopes and so I missed seeing the Salerno beaches where General Mark Clark's men so nearly were pushed back into the sea, but we must have passed by less than a mile from them.

They have missed a major eruption three weeks earlier when the great bulging shape of the smoke from the crater was a majestic and terrible sight – like that, as Pliny wrote, of a many-branching pine tree, absolutely motionless, not quite painted because it was three-dimensional but moulded in the sky, 'an utterly still and utterly menacing shape.

It spewed forth, as if in protest at the man-made destruction, its own signal of man's transient passage on this planet.' Fraser:

> *April 16*. Finally at about 10.30 am we suddenly appeared in Naples harbour out of the mist, and as we approached it was possible to tell what damage had been caused there by the shelling, bombing and German demolitions. Of course the balloons were right up and there was a bit of shooting soon after we arrived – probably a recce plane or practice. Naples stands on a hill sloping down towards the bay and harbour before it was so badly knocked about must have been a most lovely place, but the bombing and shelling has caused havoc, especially in the southern part of the town. Mount Vesuvius overlooks the city and harbour from the south side, but it was no longer erupting when we arrived.

So here they are in the war-ravaged city in April 1944. Naples deserves a whole book, if not several, of its own: no greater, more poignant an account of the conditions here is to be found than in Norman Lewis's diary, *Naples '44*. He describes starving, blind little girls between nine and twelve years from an orphanage lured by the smell of food in a restaurant being turned away by indifferent diners: 'I had clung to the comforting belief that human beings eventually come to terms with pain and sorrow. Now I understood I was wrong.'

The city had been mutilated by the Nazis before they left, both physically and culturally. The vengeance extended from burning coal stockpiles, blowing up and cutting off water supplies, dynamiting sewers, bridges, industrial and utility plants, to burning over 100,000 books in libraries. The wreckage of harbour cranes was symbolic of the destruction of Naples' mercantile and shipping power: 300 had been sabotaged or toppled over into the water.

For the highest of the high it is different. When General Mark Clark comes to Naples and asks for fish at the banquet offered to him, the Neapolitans provide, as the main course, a boiled baby manatee – formerly the most prized specimen in Naples's celebrated aquarium.

For Neapolitans food takes precedence even over love, and so love is offered for food: an estimated 42,000 women out of a nubile population of 150,000 work as prostitutes in a population 'where nine out of ten Italian girls had lost their menfolk ... either disappeared in battles, into prisoner-of-war camps, or been cut off in the North.' Otherwise, the whole population is out of work.

The Regiment has little time to experience the full impact of the devastation and horror, the endemic deprivation and starvation, the black market, and the child as well as adult prostitution. Ewart remembers that you could not leave a vehicle alone anywhere for a few minutes without losing its tyres to thieves. Henry Uxbridge's first view of Naples shocks him deeply: 'Naples was blind, there were no windows with any glass in them ... a horror of barbed wire enclosures behind which hordes of starved children, all fat bellied, unhappy, miserable. This is our first moment of arrival in this great country of Italy. None of us is allowed to help in any way we could.' Fraser is more sanguine:

Now as regards the destruction itself it was definitely nothing like as bad as I had been led to believe from the news. The papers led us to believe that there was very little left of this lovely spot, either harbour or city but that is quite wrong. Naturally the harbour has had the worst time, and the buildings near it but from the north the town is by no means all that badly hit about.

In the dock areas, almost all the houses are gutted but everywhere rubble and many wharfs and sidings in the docks have been blown up. There is one hospital ship lying close in, completely on her side, a total wreck and three other smallish ships lying on the bottom, all useless in their present condition. There is also half submerged wreckage in the centre harbour ...

There were about 6 British destroyers and 2 cruisers, one Greek cruiser, and a lot of smaller stuff. Of course they have had time to clear away quite a lot of rubble and wrecks so when the Germans left I should imagine the harbour must have been in a worse condition. The destruction to the Naples marshalling yards is immense – we saw this on 15 April. But boats go in and out continuously now and there are plenty of small craft about. The most noticeable thing naturally is the lack of local inhabitants round the dock areas, but we cannot expect to see people where there are no buildings for men to live in, so that was only natural.

We saw lots of jeeps and American lorries about, and plenty of 5th Army men, 'Yanks' I would say! So much for the harbour area itself, we got off the boat at 2.45pm and having shed our packs in the main street for transport by lorry. We set out on a quiet route march,

arriving at the stage camp at 7.00pm. We marched right through the
town, and the things that impressed me most were – Lack of shops – I saw
a few grocers, they were the best – No tram service. People seemed quite
happy. Numbers of Italian soldiers about doing very little! Great amount
of American traffic.

Fraser is an optimist; his glass is always half full. The stage camp is
outside the city. The next day:

Heavy dew, but sun soon comes through. What a lovely change from
sand. Breakfast at nine with troops. Italians all over the camp selling wal-
nuts and apples. Tidied up in morning. Bought two books on the Italian
language, which I am going to try and learn. Meals 'al fresco' Not in a
mess tent. Bed at 9.00pm. Cold at night.

They are now less than 100 miles from one of the world's main
battle-fronts – the line (the Gustav Line) east of the Rapido River,
and the approach to Rome blocked by Monte Cassino still held by the
Germans. A sober assessment of what is in store can be taken from Karl
Marlantes, a writer who fought in Vietnam, whose observation applies
equally to the European war in 1944 – and to present-day Afghanistan:

War ... blows away the illusion of safety from death. Some random projectile can kill you no matter how good a soldier you are. Escaping death
and injury in modern warfare is much more a matter of luck – or grace
– than skill, and this is a significant difference from primitive warfare. In a
combat situation you wake up from sleep instantly aware that this could
be the last time you awake, simultaneously grateful you're alive and
scared shitless because you are still in the same situation. Most combat
veterans keep this awareness – that death is just around the corner. We
know that when we drive the freeway to work we could be dead within
the next hour. It's just that the odds have changed greatly in our favour
from when we were in combat. It's the difference in the odds of getting
killed that makes combat a noticeable experience of one's mortality and
going to work or the freeway an unnoticed one.

It is at once apparent to Ewart that while he will have his private fears
and doubts, he must not communicate them to his troop. A thin line

divides this from deliberate deception. It is the dispassionate attitude of the leader he has to have, which defines not only his relationship with his men but also with his fellow officers. He is to become emotionally involved with both, for without this few men will respond, and few will work to the best of their ability. With him, you feel, grip is vital: grip on oneself, grip on one's soldiers, and grip on the situation. Ewart's men have to have confidence in his professional ability, and at the same time trust him as a man. It is a hard call, given he is not yet twenty. As is well known, newcomers in battle suffer the highest casualties.

CHAPTER FIVE

THE MARCH UP THE HILL

'What the hell are you doing, Mr Wellesley? Your job is commanding your troop, not popping off the enemy.'

Squadron Leader to Lt Wellesley in the Syrian desert, 1942

All the men of the Regiment remember the march out of Naples to their first camp in Italy, a march which is an affront to a highly mechanized unit who have now been training for months with their armoured vehicles. Valerian Douro has hardly any impressions of Naples. 'I was sorry I wasn't going to see my wife for a long time. We marched an awful long way for us unfit cavalrymen to a camp about 10 miles out of Naples. In the meantime lots was happening, the main British advances in Italy were up the west coast, some on the east too. We had the role of going up the spine, the centre, most unsuitable for armoured cars used to the freedom of the desert.' He is apprehensive about going into the line on the European mainland because it will not be at all like desert warfare, in open terrain with no civilians about, 'who made warfare so messy'. It is that steep hill that Van Ammel recalls most:

We weren't trained as infantry and hadn't marched anywhere for years. Troops coming back down the hill in carriers and lorries yelled out, 'What's it like back in Knightsbridge?' You could see the men were seething with rage, they'd been out there for five years. They thought we were 'Pinkies' – people straight from England, not even sunburned. They

70

were shouting at us as we trudged up the bloody hill. We got to Caserta and took over the Royals armoured cars. We went off across in these armoured cars to the Adriatic side. No sooner had we got there than we were dismounted again and turned into infantry.

Clearly the memory has clouded, for the first day's march to Afrigola staging camp is seven miles but felt like more. Here they stay for two days, march to Caserta, and catch a train at 9am on the 15th for Ponte Cagnano (where they are expected at 1600 hrs). The men travel in cattle trucks, the officers in a 2nd-class coach. The forty miles takes seventeen hours rather than the expected seven, and they arrive at 1am where transport is waiting to take them to the camp. Three and a half hours' sleep is all they get. Here, while issued with a full complement of vehicles, they are now training in patrolling both by night and day on foot, ominously, 'in case the regiment should be employed in a dismounted role'.

The new camp is 10 miles east of Salerno and here the Regiment is settled in for the rest of April. They patrol, swim in the sea or local streams and receive their first mail for a month (Fraser receives fifteen letters). It is a strange moment of peace, even stranger because they are less than 100 miles from one of the biggest killing fields of the war – the continuing Allied assaults on Monte Cassino to open the way to Rome. Fraser is sitting

... just outside my tent on this lovely spring afternoon, in our new camp. I feel that I must just take up my pen and write down what this beautiful country is like in short form; so that eventually, when I am allowed to say where I am, I shall not leave anything out, for those who must be so eagerly awaiting my news at home.

Italy is certainly a most beautiful country, and we have had the luck to take over a camp in a valley ... that is completely unspoilt by the war which swept by here, not many months ago.

Our camp is situated in the grounds of an old Italian mansion, and we have the house too, which serves as the mess, orderly room and some of the senior officers' quarters. All round us are mountains, with trees and houses dotted about their sides and the grounds themselves are mostly vineyards, with sprouting wheat and trees of many description. The apple blossom is lovely. Round these vineyards and trees fly the birds whose

71

song is increasing, and lots of butterflies, not to mention the bumble bees. The whole atmosphere of the place is completely peaceful, and I have not heard even an aeroplane yet. This really is remarkable when you consider that the American 5th Army is still outside Cassino, less than 100 miles to our north. But there is nothing to spoil the peace of this spot.

The continual hum of the men's conversation, one whistling while he cleans his buttons or washes his socks, does not disturb the peace – only the armoured cars and lorries, in their long straight rows remind us that we are not here for pleasure but on a special task.

Ewart has the same experience. On Wednesday, April 19 he plans to visit the opera, *The Barber of Seville*, playing in Salerno; but Porchey fails to arrange transport, so in spite of eating an early dinner he doesn't go. John is reading Tolstoy's *War and Peace*, and finds it sheer bliss walking in the countryside, which reminds him so much of home. He hikes alone to the top of a hill: 'I could see the whole of the Salerno Bay where the landings took place. Met an Italian shepherd who gave me his stick. I realise so well what the difference is between the important and unimportant things but I can never keep a singleness of purpose – nor can other people as far as I can see.' He hears of the death of a fellow officer. Duncan Boulton is missing, believed killed: 'First class man, now first of my squad has been killed.'

Douro has given himself a very personal mission. His cousin, formerly the Earl of Mornington and known as Morny, who had inherited the Dukedom on his father's death in December 1941, took part in the Salerno landing in September. It was then, prior to Normandy, the biggest amphibious operation of the War, in which 170,000 men took part.

Eighty-five Allied vessels of the invasion fleet were hit in the Bay of Salerno, mainly by a guided missile called Fritz, and many men died. The setback was such that Churchill suggested he fly to the beachhead to bolster morale, while Eisenhower almost lost his command in the face of an expected retreat, finally avoided in the reduced beachhead by a devastating off-shore bombardment of the German positions by Allied ships.

A captain in No 2 Commando, Morny was in the spearhead of the attack, and in the thick of the fighting in the early morning six days after they landed. Scaling a hill at the head of his troops with his Sergeant Major, he lost his life in hand-to-hand combat as his assault failed.

Douro saw his cousin as a naturally brave type, carrying, as Jane Wellesley writes, 'the burden of his complicated legacy', which at first he had been reluctant to embrace: 'We all went off to war without really thinking about the sacrifices that were demanded of us. We were doing our duty and it was not something we really analysed. But when friends and comrades were killed the enormity of it all came home to us. And Morny *chose* to fight in a unit that suffered far higher losses than any other part of the army. And he really did die a hero's death.'

In the lull before Douro is to engage in his own battle destiny he finds a jeep and drives to look for Morny's grave, either in the newly dug Salerno war cemetery or on the small hill known as the Pimple. Unbeknown to him, Jack Churchill, Morny's commanding officer, had already searched, and found on the hill-top Morny's badly burned body together with his Sergeant Major's, both hastily buried under six inches of earth. Churchill carried the two men's remains to temporary interment in a grass square on Salerno's outskirts, from which they were later removed to the official cemetery. Ultimately there are to be 37 Commonwealth cemeteries in Italy, where 38,000 casualties of the Italian campaign rest.

Douro had experienced his own baptism of fire earlier in the desert. In 1941, when west of Baghdad, his A Squadron had moved to five miles west of Baghdad, ready to help free the city from the Iraqi Army's rebellion and restore British control, as well as to rescue the captives in the Embassy. The terrain was flooded, the Iraqi army well dug in, with 18 pounders shelling 1HCR's position.

He was saddened to see a number of bee eaters that were nesting in holes in the banks of the cutting lying dead on the road, killed by shell fire. He picked one up and 'it was of a different type to that with which we were familiar in Palestine. I looked it up in my bird book and found it was a type found in Asia and India.'

B Squadron was sent to reconnoitre – dismounted and in force – towards the Shia Mosque of Khadinam with its golden dome but was repulsed by heavy machine-gun fire, which killed one man, Trooper Shone. HQ sent Douro with his troop to recover Shone's body and pin-point the position of the machine guns. He marched two miles, after a reprimand from his Colonel to spread out his men, to a position near Khadinam and within 200 yards of Shone's body.

Setting a section to his right and to the left and some men behind him, Valerian, his Corporal of Horse Maxted, his soldier servant Pearson and two troopers stood up to advance in arrowhead formation – with Valerian as the arrowhead.

This was a classic dilemma for the well-trained officer. Obviously he had to set an example and always lead from the front, although not everyone did. Yet if he grew over-eager and got himself killed or wounded, his previous training and his responsibility to the men he led would be thrown away. In fact he would be letting down his Regiment.

As Valerian walked, he kept his eyes glued on the ridge ahead hoping he would get some warning if the enemy was still in position. It was very still and hot, the sun glinted on the golden dome of the Mosque that rose above the roofs of the village ahead of them. But there was a disturbing and eerie silence:

> When we had gone a hundred yards I was beginning to think we had got away with it and was wondering how we were going to get Shone's body back. Like most pre-war troopers he was a big man and we had come unencumbered with a stretcher. It therefore came almost as a surprise when a veritable storm of machine gun fire suddenly descended on us. We tried to wriggle our puny bodies in the hard unyielding sand and just waited for this terrible cacophony of sound to stop. After what seemed an age but was probably not much more than a minute, the fire seemed to slacken and I raised my head slightly to see if I could see anything. There was a small cloud of dust at two points on the forward edge of the village and I reckoned from the rate of fire that we were up against two pairs of Vickers machine guns firing from enfilading positions dug in on the forward edge of the village.

Valerian knew, having served with a machine gun platoon, that these were British machine guns fired by British-trained Iraqis. He could assess the range and fixed lines of fire, and see they had walked into the 'beaten zone'. His troop responded with covering fire, which helped reduce the fire, but they had to retreat with Shone's body. Fortunately there was no counter-attack as they began to fall back one by one. Maxted was sent first as they sheltered behind dunes to get more covering fire. He stood up, all six feet three inches of him, brushed the sand off his uniform and

> ... marched erect and straight with his rifle at the short trail across that hundred yards of desert as if he was on the parade ground at Windsor. It

was a magnificently defiant gesture ... Whatever his own feelings were, and he must have been as afraid as we were, he wasn't going to show it. The movement had triggered off more firing and I watched him go back to the ridge as the bullets flicked up the sand all round him with a full heart and a prayer on my lips. Once he was sent back I sent the others back one by one. They kept well over to the left as I looked back and soon Maxted had the rifles of the section on the ridge firing away at the enemy positions in the village. It was now my turn and I stood up feeling rather lonely and with an uncomfortable feeling in my back as I tried rather unsuccessfully to emulate my Corporal of Horse. However, all went well and I arrived back to find Maxted as cool as a cucumber giving fire orders as if he was on the ranges at Pirbright.

Valerian now had to follow, feeling lonely and uncomfortable while continuing to pin-point the machine guns and reboot himself to observe the enemy position:

The little ridge soon disappeared and I had a twenty-yard gap before I could reach the next dune. I reckoned, with the Vickers difficult to traverse quickly, I had little to fear ... [But] I was now the target of enemy rifles. In Wild West films, as the hero dodges from rock to rock with outlaws, Red Indians or whatever firing at him, the bullets make a rather satisfactory whine as they go off into space. The reality ... as I remembered from my days in the butts at Bisley and Pirbright ... [is that a] bullet passing fairly close makes a most unpleasant crack as it breaks the sound barrier, particularly if it's just over one's head! The same fusillade of shots followed me each time I dodged from dune to dune ... there was within me a little pang of exhilaration rather like jumping several big fences out hunting.

Fortunately, they were facing inaccurate Iraqi and not German fire. All his troop survived unscathed. On arrival at base when he reported the heavy fire his surprised Colonel commented drily, 'We didn't hear anything.' His Intelligence Officer, who debriefed him, said 'You look all in – have a whisky.' He had been spared, but his cousin Morny had not. Douro's daughter reflects on one outcome:

Morny, who had spent his whole life preparing to inherit the dukedom carried the title for less than two years; my father, the son of a younger son, never expected to become Duke, but from 16 September 1943 the responsibilities of his life were mapped out by the legacy which accompanies the title. I wonder whether he might concede that part of him wishes that he had not inherited it; but in any case, the answer could never be a simple 'yes' or 'no'.

Leaving Salerno, Douro returns to his squadron. Thirty miles north of Naples lay Caserto, the Allied GHQ, which 1HCR has passed through without stopping. In stark and outrageous contrast to the Salerno struggle, Caserta was a Bourbon palace with twelve hundred rooms, a theatre with forty boxes, a marble staircase and courtyards to rival Versailles, now the HQ of Clark's Fifth Army and Alexander's 15th Army Group.

It came to house, as the campaign grew and intensified, 15,000 polyglot Allied staff, a miniature city that rapidly became like a royal court, a 'looking glass world' of intrigue, fleshpots and even a 'colony' built for generals called Cascades. 'One does not hate on a full stomach and on hot baths,' observed one officer, while the engineers of exclusive luxury for the high command, beefed: 'The feeling of them is that they came here for the purpose of winning a war. The building of summer houses doesn't fall under this category.'

Eight thousand carrier pigeons in twenty-two lofts contributed to the numbers housed in this parody of the Pentagon, their cooing rivalled by the noisy nightingales in the surrounding verdure. General Clark laconically commented, 'Never before in the history of warfare have so few been commanded by so many.' The quarrels, disagreements, accusations, and self-justifications of those commanders have filled and fuelled many books and debates.

We come to the tipping point. On Monday, May 1, Ewart notes:

Patrolled and went for route march in morning. In afternoon did Bren and Tommy gun training. Conference at 5.30 saying we are moving tomorrow. Packed up kit. Everyone seems very happy and quite oblivious of what is about to happen. Was writing letters in evening when Colonel walked in and talked solidly for over half an hour – he appeared far more apprehensive than anyone else.

Tuesday, May 2:

> Rev 5.30 but left at 9.30 after hanging round for hours. I travelled in
> 3 Tonners with troops Journey of 80 miles to starting area. Area very
> bombed. Apparently we are going to 5th corps which consists of 4th, 8th,
> Indian Divs and a force called D Force consisting of central India Horse to
> which we are going to be attached.

Wednesday:

> Further 150 miles through Termoli and Vasto to the Sangro. Then went
> into a little village called Archi ... On the way thought of all the various
> things that could happen to us and I reckon that we certainly were not
> properly trained in what we are about to do but by being intelligent we
> should quickly learn as we go along.

Again it is Malcolm Fraser, less questioning than Ewart, who provides a
more comprehensive record. They are now on the other side from where
the big battles are being fought:

> Leave camp area at 6.30am. pass through Foggia, San Saverno, Termoli
> and Vasto. The Adriatic was lovely when we first saw it from the hill above
> Termoli. Road from Termoli to Vasto very bad; saw several German tanks
> (derelict) on the side of the road. Reached Vasto about 2.30pm. Half hour
> lunch halt, then straight on to Archi which is our camp area. Archi over-
> looks the river Sangro and commands a grand view for about 20 miles
> right up to those enormous snow capped mountains called *Montagne
> della Maiella*, in the foothills of which are the German positions. Casoli is
> about 6 miles in front of us; Orsogno to the North just visible.
>
> We came right down to the Sangro bridge on our way to Archi. It
> has 16 foundations and is an enormous length. The river itself is at the
> moment very low, but when in flood as it was when the 8th Army had to
> cross it, it must have been a most terrible task. The Sangro Valley is about
> 5 miles across.

Both the Sangro River and Casoli have been the scene earlier of terrible carnage, of advances won in the face of the most bitter, bloody and
determined resistance.

We are to take over a part of the line held at the moment by a unit called 'D' Force. This stretches from a place called Fara, about 5 miles S.W. of Casoli to a place called Lama, about 3 miles S.W. of Fara, both towered over by these enormous Maiella Mountains (10,000 feet) – B Sqn is to take Fara, and A Sqn Lama – RHQ at Civitella, about 1 mile East from Fara.

Lama is definitely the most likely place to have any trouble, as the Germans are just south of a town called Taranta. This town is patrolled by both sides continuously.

Units on our right – The 9th Manchesters are at Paloubaro and the 4th Indian Div the other side of them. To our left the K.R.G.'s [King's Royal Dragoons] at Monteverodi, stretching south west.

D Force is commanded by Lieutenant Colonel Hunt, later the conqueror of Mount Everest, who, to some officers' annoyance, deems that every patrol that goes out, however small, must have an officer in charge. This is, Van Ammel says, 'dangerous and wearing. We were raw recruits as far as that warfare was concerned. We had armoured cars wrapped up around us, protecting us. Mind you, there were people couldn't bear the thought of an armoured car because you get trapped and burned, but there were people who couldn't bear the thought of being an infantry man – I was one of those.'

On May 4 they dig themselves in, not as an armoured car regiment, but as infantry; their vehicles are parked to the east, a manoeuvre which gives rise to considerable grief – for we are now into early May, and a good grain crop is expected. Van Ammel:

> Douro had to choose locations, and to choose from a military point of view the ideal was an open hilly farm. The unfortunate thing was the family's corn was so high, and our armoured car squadron went over it. I remember the Italian family who were looking forward to living off it for the next year; they were on their knees praying us not to do that ... It was hell! The men in their armoured cars felt that, felt acutely, they fell over themselves to take them tins of bully, anything they could find. We had to leave the cars and go on foot.

Their transport is parked out of range of the Hun artillery in Lama, east of the Sangro River, and they prepare to go forward on foot to make contact with the enemy. Digging their slit trenches they are now, says Ewart on May 4

> ... approximately 9½ miles from the nearest Germans. In the afternoon, short route march then short lecture by Colonel. He had just come back from the front and said that two squadrons will go up to the front almost immediately and the 3rd will train in armoured work for a week and then relieve. A and B going up first and Tony is going for a Recce tomorrow. He hinted that two troops would be going together and that [Neville] Brayne-Nicholls would be given a job. So it leaves chances of going rather slighter than most considering I am 2nd junior subaltern. Although I think it is far better to let things work themselves out ... I would feel rather disappointed if I did not go.

To the west, or in front of the Regiment, lies the enemy. Although the Luftwaffe was reduced to flying only 50 sorties a day over Italy, which means 1HCR are never attacked from the air, and although the Germans suffered shortages in men and materials, the advantage in that terrain of what General Alexander called 'ridge and furrow' stays with the defender.

To the south-west of where the Regiment is dug in, huge and successive waves of attack try to break the grip on Cassino. Similarly, in this 'unprofitable' Adriatic sector with no strategic objective, Generals Montgomery, Clark, Alexander and the rest learn to their fury that superiority in tanks and guns, fighter and bomber squadrons, brings little advantage. These are countered by adverse weather, abominable terrain, and a grimly determined force of battle-seasoned professionals with artillery and anti-tank, hand-held Faust rockets.

'Watch where you step,' Clark's headquarters advises, 'and have no curiosity at all. You can follow our battalions [going north] by the blood-stained leggings, the scattered equipment, and the bits of bodies where men had been blown up,' the US 168th Infantry reports. 'Castrators' or 'nutcrackers' fire a bullet upward when an unwitting soldier steps on the pressure plate. 'Shoe', or *Schu* mines, built mostly of wood, prove nearly impossible to detect. Enemy sappers mine and booby-trap doorknobs and desk drawers, grapevines and haystacks, apples on the tree and bodies on the ground – whether they are Italian or German, Tommy or Yank. Two chaplains lose legs trying to bury the dead above the Volturno.

'A man's foot is usually blown loose at the ankle, leaving the man-gled foot dangling on shredded tendons,' notes an army physician in his diary. 'Additional puncture wounds to both legs and groin make the agony worse.' A combat medic later writes, 'Even though you'd give them a shot or two of morphine, they would still scream.' In minefields 'an old man thinks of his eyes and a young man grabs for his balls.' Some 100,000 SCR-625 mine detectors – dubbed 'manhole covers on a stick' – prove useless in the rain and become 'befuddled' by the iron ore and shell fragments in the Italian soil. 'Canine mine detectors', dogs, also fail miserably.

Against them is pitted the technical and industrial killing efficiency of a superior German army in front of Rome. They flood the valleys, mine the roads, detonate the airfields, blow up the bridges, snipe from superior ground invisible in snow-suits. Allied soldiers in no-man's-land see and feel the enemy is everywhere watching and about to strike, and death and maiming await them at every twist and turn of their advance.

Meanwhile, the Allied commanders bicker and quarrel among them-selves like the Greeks in their tents before Troy. Montgomery reflects on the stalemate: 'The Americans do not understand how to fight the Germans ... They do not understand the great principles of surprise and concentration.' In his private memoirs he castigates Alexander, who 'has very little idea as to how to operate armies in the field. When he has a conference of commanders, which is very seldom, it is a lamentable spectacle ... No one gets any orders, and we all do what we like.' He wor-ries 'We may be led into further troubles in 1944 and will not finish off the war cleanly.' His conclusion is that the Italian war is 'a detestable thing, untidy and hot.'

The Regiment is far from 'untidy' but spread out between the villages of Archi and Perano. Facing it is the *Della Maiella* mountain range, with its massive peaks of *Monte Cavallo, Monte Acquaviva* and *Monte Amaro,* the highest of the trio at 3,195 metres, over 9,000 feet. At the foot of this mass runs the Aventino River in a valley with winding roads and railway line approximately north-south. As the enemy, two battalions of infantry with artillery, has withdrawn to the high ground above the river, he has worked out accurately where to range his fire at the promi-nent features along the valley that holds five villages or small towns – from north to south, Faro and Civitella, Lama, Taranto, Lattopalena and finally, the crucial one, Palena itself.

Because Lama (and the Regiment will be advancing south) is in no-man's-land and West of Fallascoso, they can expect to be shelled. But the Regiment's role in battle is to reconnoitre, and you cannot reconnoitre in a vacuum. You probe, and cover forward fighting units as their ears and eyes, to identify weak spots, observe and learn the intentions of the enemy. You delay and harass with involvement or, in the huntsman's tradition, when you have spotted the quarry, you pursue. Above all, you listen and are in touch. It is a strange, even sometimes chivalric role in brutal, modern warfare: just to challenge and to remain in contact with the enemy. No blood lust, no triumphalism, no revenge – it calls for a dispassionate approach.

To this end Palena, lying directly in the shadow of Monte Amaro, or Bitter Mountain, now in German hands, is the key to what must be done.

CHAPTER SIX

ARRIVAL AT PALENA – BAPTISM OF FIRE

To the man in the field a minor patrol may for him contain more of a personal drama than any great battle. For an Intelligence Officer the day in which the presence of a new formation is discussed can be of greater note than the victory to which the discovery leads.

Geoffrey Cox, Intelligence Officer, New Zealand 2nd Division

'When Winston Churchill said that Italy was "the soft underbelly of Europe" he could not have been thinking in terms of military tactics,' Herbert says. 'There is nothing soft about the Apennines as a terrain for war. They are an attacker's nightmare, and the defender's dream. To none was this quality more obvious than to us, an armoured car regiment essentially created for the fast pursuit of a retreating enemy; but with roads and bridges blown, the valleys mined, and the Germans commanding the high ground of their chosen lines of defence, there was simply no role for our armoured vehicles. With no time for training we were thrown into action on foot as mountain troops.'

Kesselring has already judged the superior forces of the democratic nations ranged against him with superior firepower to be little better than militia. They would be paying heavily for their inexperience and poorer training with vastly greater casualties. Only attrition is the answer to defeating the Germans, and they are slowly rolled back, but they hardly waver in their dogged, quasi-religious devotion to the Führer, and to Germany. Nothing, it seems, will deter them from defending unto death. As 1944 wears on, they have more men under arms, including vassal units of every race from countries they have overrun, than ever before.

Through 'Ultra', or the cracking of the Enigma Code, the Allies know in advance what the next German moves and strategy will be, but with the poor communications they have between them, often this knowledge does not reach the commanders in the field, or if it does they still make the wrong decisions.

> During the night 6/7 May CIH [Central India Horse] reported Germans to have withdrawn from Palena and were following up. Therefore hand over to the Regt would be postponed for 24hrs. A and B Sqn Ldrs continued their recce of areas to be taken over.
> 1300: A Sqn ordered to move up immediately to Lama and take over from B Sqn CIH and patrol South to re-est contact with the enemy.
> RHQ and B Sqn to move the following day to Lama. By last light a standing patrol from A Sqn was est in Palena 1175. No contact with enemy.

The terse War Office report frames Fraser's personal take on what A Squadron find on moving in:

May 8, 9, 1944. The Bosch really are devils. I was one of the first patrols to enter Palena after the Bosch left it on the night of May 7th/8th so found it almost exactly as they left it. About 80% of houses are useless, many have walls standing but others also are completely flat. Much of this is due to shelling, but before they left the Germans blew up many of them with mines. The mess inside the houses is terrible. It looked just as if the Germans had walked into them, turned everything upside down, taken everything they wanted and then pushed off. Several houses reek of dead bodies under the rubble.

***

Eight months or so earlier, before Italy changed sides and the savage suppression of this mountainous area began, Palena had been a charming and extremely pretty town with a wealth of old houses and a historical tradition centred on the life of Saint Falco.

Legend has it that St Falco was born in the second half of the tenth century in Taverna. He left his family as a young man to retreat to the hermitage of Pescara under the supervision of the Abbot Hilarion, head of the Basilian monks. Evading Saracen invasions and looting, Abbot Hilarion and his brothers, including St Falco, bought land near Aventino. They built a small church and monastic cells and devoted their lives to meditation and helping others. After the death of his abbot, St Falco set off as a pilgrim to Rome and arrived at Palena, where he stopped to rest. Here he settled in a small hermitage on a mountain outside. The local people all soon knew of his holiness and the power given him by God to expel evil spirits that possessed individuals.

On January 13, in some year in the second half of the tenth century, the bell of the hermitage started ringing and some young people went to the mountain to find St Falco. They discovered him lying lifeless on a table between two candles, one at his head and the other at his feet. His body was brought to and buried in the Church of Sant' Egidio Abate, where his body, it is recorded, exhaled a sweet perfume. On August 29, 1383, the body of St Falco was transferred to the Mother Church of St Anthony.

When, much later, he was canonised as Palena's patron saint, a half-length statue of him was cast in silver, inside which they carefully stored the relic of his sacred skull. Each year on January 13, and on the following Sunday, this is exposed to the faithful in a public ceremony; this also happens on August 29 in memory of the relocation of his relics from the Church of Sant' Egidio to that of St Anthony.

Life for the 3000 Palenesi before the terrible events of September 1943 was peaceful, productively rural and buoyantly Italian. On September 8 the cobblestones of the main *corso* echoed with the crunch of marching German troops as they occupied the town hall. 'They arrived in the dark. Children were among the first to see a long line of headlights across the Maiella Mountains. And very soon the ravaged houses and bombed streets of their little home town would be a children's playground,' laments an Italian witness.

Lettopalena, just north of Palena on the River Aventino, was destroyed first. The Germans got there on October 11, 1943. The SS registered all able-bodied men and forced them to build fortifications as part of the Gustav Line. Then they ordered that when these were finished the village should be destroyed. They evicted the people at gunpoint, and on November 19 and 20 the ancient medieval village was obliterated by mines. Not even the Abbey of Santa Maria di Monteplanizio was spared.

In February 1944, three months later, about 200 Lettopalenesi tried to return. Heedless of danger and of the Nazi presence they found shelter in their destroyed homes, occupying every cave, stone hut and haystack. The Germans rounded them up and took them to Palena, where they were jailed for four days.

At four in the morning they were released. Snow, which already covered the ground in a thick blanket, was falling heavily. On foot, escorted by armed guards, the group set out for the town of Rocca Pia. During the long hours of the march they suffered extreme cold and fatigue, and deaths followed; children were the first. The group arrived at Rocca Pia at midnight; fifteen died on the 20-hour march.

Other refugees from Lettopalena moved into empty stables in Palena belonging to their relatives (kinship ties between neighbouring villages were strong). But the Germans kicked the relatives out of their homes and moved in, so there would be two extended families living in one stable. They pretended to have TB to keep the Germans at a distance. Then the Allies bombed Palena. One family hid in the crypt of St Anthony's with St Falco's statue and survived the heavy bombing. To preserve it, the statue was taken and built into the wall of the church.

The Palenesi took different paths into exile. Some were marched out by the Germans and during their journey in the snow one woman gave birth on the mountainside. A young boy died of exposure while his mother tried to save her elderly parents. Others hid in the cemetery morgue, their home for many weeks, while in mountain huts and caves survival got so desperate in the freezing cold that some were forced back to their decimated dwellings. They hid food such as bottles of tomato sauce down wells, and lived on wild plants. The Germans stole all their winter supplies, their salamis, their flour and vegetables. They seized food and looted shops in the commercial centres.

They also raped. One woman, Rosa Del Bene, who in 2012 is on the path to beatification, threw herself out of her bedroom window to avoid German soldiers who had stormed upstairs to rape her. In another episode a large number of people were imprisoned in a room where they struggled to breathe; here a baby was born but later died. Terror and reprisal became the order of the day and many were the tales of humiliation, desperation, and death.

Soon, all along the Aventino valley skirmishes began between resistance patriots, who formed the famous Maiella Brigade, and German units. Both sides suffered heavy casualties. The skirmishes ended with the Italians fleeing into the Maiella range, with mass executions of those caught. In various towns and villages there were uprisings, which were savagely suppressed. One of the first bloody clashes and scene of the first German reprisals was at Lanciano, October 5–6, 1943. Groups of young people rose and fought for two days in the streets. The uprising may have seemed futile, but finding weapons from somewhere the insurgents kept up fire from windows and balconies.

During it the Germans captured a bearded young man, and to extract the names of patriot leaders tied him head down to a pole in the square. Angry at his stubborn silence a German soldier hollowed out his eyes with his bayonet, then slit his belly open. Many more were mown down by machine gun fire while the first twelve young men that came to hand were seized and shot. Lanciano was later decorated with a gold medal for its bravery in resistance.

On November 3, to consolidate the Gustav Line, the Germans had ordered the evacuation of Palena: many small townships suffered the same fate. In the following months, wherever the Germans built defences there were throngs of men, women, elderly and children, trudging down broken roads to the valleys loaded with mattresses, furniture, baskets, parcels and bags of all kinds, from which fell books, tins, cartons, utensils, work tools, photos, balls of string, braids of garlic and onion. Men disappeared under huge loads of crates and boxes, swollen and knotted with rags and blankets.

Young ladies from 'comfortable' homes, now barefoot and dishevelled, dragged bundles worthy of the most solid laundresses. People scoured the countryside looking for barns, caves, burrows of *allocarvisi*. The farms, even their attics, were full of friends and relatives, acquaintances and strangers who made use of every hole. A forkful of straw, a bundle of clothes – and a bed was ready. Barter was the order of the day. A kilo of beans was worth a pack of 'Popular' (cigarettes), a litre of oil could be bartered for five pounds of sugar. Matches reached a staggering price.

All through autumn and winter there is attack and counter-attack by the patriots, who are sometimes informed on by Italian fascists and ambushed. This is civil war, a guerrilla campaign, and a protracted German-Allied conflict all taking place at once: the most horrific scenario that can be imagined.

On January 13, 1944 the by-now mainly empty Palena is bombed again by Anglo-American planes, reducing the centre to rubble, destroying St Anthony's, leaving only the bell tower standing. Grimly committed to slowing down the advance of the 8th Army, the Germans have destroyed everything they can, bridges, railway lines, roads, every domestic house, razing towns and villages and as in their scorched earth policy in Russia, leaving only minefields and rubble. They have had plenty of practice.

It is this zone of horror and devastation that Malcolm Fraser of A Squadron enters on May 8, 1944. Next morning:

P.T. at 6.15. Still very windy, found shaving very difficult. 9.00am Sqn parade and Troop route marches. I took my troop with Valerian across S.W. from Archi – come in at 12.45 to be told that we are to move off at 3pm and take over the part of the line allotted to us. A risk but we got off about 3.30pm. Went to Lama in Tp 3 – tonner where I was immediately sent to the Colonel, who gave me orders for a 36 hr patrol with 1 NCO and one guerrilla. A bit of a shake!! Repack kit in Lama, taking only small pack, arms and sleeping bag with one blanket, glasses and my compass. Set off at 7.30 pm down the road. Our destination was Lettopalena, about 4½ miles away. The march took 3 hours exactly, during which time we forded a river (bridge being blown) up to our thighs. Several went under, my map case was lost by my servant which was very annoying. Arrived in Lettopalena 10.20pm to find John Shaw and Tony already there. Found a guerrilla about ¾ hour later for patrol, but luckily the task had been changed – recce road south of Palena as far as possible, being back by first light. Left at 11.30pm in a soaking wet condition – patrol uneventful: Came in about 6.00am but walked a long way. Palena in a very bad mess: literally ransacked by the Bosch and blown up as well. Absolutely deserted when we went through.

In Lama before he goes down to Palena, Douro has a bizarre encounter. He spots some Pointer puppies in a house and wants to see if he can purchase one. He climbs to the first floor and here he finds an extremely pretty girl, elegantly dressed, in a room bare of everything but a bed and chair. 'I went and sat on the chair and she sat on the bed – a few paces away – and asked me, in good English, if I could help her – I wondered what was coming!' The tale she told, as often in these encounters between Italian women and British soldiers, turned out to be lengthy. The girl and her brother had been suspected of being fascists. The brother was now in jail; she wanted Valerian to intercede on his behalf. Ever the gentleman, Douro noted down the details and promised to do what he could, but she must have sensed that he had some niggling doubts about her story. 'I went towards the door to leave but she stood with her back firmly against it and put her arms round my neck – stay with me, she pleaded.' He was not to be persuaded, so he gave her a chaste kiss on the forehead and left saying that he would do what he could. He joined his comrades down in the street waiting for him unaware of the encounter. 'I thought I had got away with it until they all started to laugh. And when I looked up to the first floor window of the house. She was leaning out and waving with her luscious bosom on full display!'

When Douro reaches Taranta, the next village, he asks Gavin Astor to check up on the brother. And here he finds out that not only is he a leading fascist, but also that his sister the glamorous seductress has been the mistress of the German commandant.

'The night I entered Palena,' says Douro, almost repeating Fraser, 'it reminded me of a place of the dead. The only occupants were three cats and a dog. Deathly silence reigning, and now and again there would be a most awful crash of debris falling in, then dead silence again. It was most eerie. We kept a wary eye out for booby traps, but luckily did not find any.'

Fraser's troop early next day occupies two houses commanding quite a good view of the rest of the town: 'Two of the few that had not been blown up or destroyed. We made use of all the tables and chairs etc. we could, but it was pathetic to see all the family belongings lying about among the rubble.' The road is blown up very badly on the north side, which stops any wheeled vehicles from entering the town from there.

Palena is high up, and the Scotch mist this morning made us very wet. Had troop breakfast at 7.00am. Tp and Sqn HQ's in houses, about the only ones left standing with a roof on. Very nice inside, once they had been cleaned out. Lit fires to dry blankets, clothes etc. My feet are very sore indeed from all the walking yesterday and last night.

Afternoon walk all round section positions O.P.'s etc, changing several things round, as an attack may be expected. Billets quite comfortable. Rations a bit short, but water ok.

The Regiment is not equipped for mountain warfare, unlike the enemy, and much of the patrolling is above the snow line, dangerous and demanding. John Shaw gives a good idea of what it is like:

> At 2030 hours I set out with Cpl Hawkins, Martinelli & Dode & Lamb, a rare mixture. We were all very tired and I for one very nervy. We went slowly down the road halting often when we all dozed in spite of the cold damp of the fog which had come down. We confirmed Lamb's report as we came to 7 various points. At 2030 we lay up off the road to await first light. At first light [on 10 May] we moved on uphill to get an OP [Observation Post] if possible to see the Staz. di Palena [Palena Station]. We got one but not to see the station, but we could see the German sentry at the cross roads and also an OP on the opposite hill. We stopped there an hour and then went on to try and gain the ridge ahead from which we should have seen the station. In getting there we were shelled inaccurately and having been seen we went back to Palena to report. I thought it was an unsatisfactory patrol but we got congratulated for good work.

Shaw hasn't slept for three days. He is, according to the WO Diary, 'forced to withdraw'. By now two troops of A Squadron, and Squadron HQ are in Palena. On May 10 at 10.30 hrs 31 shells fall on Palena without causing casualties, and an Artillery Mountain battery takes up its position just north of Palena to defend them. They are sending out constant patrols to recce and determine where the Germans are. Although engineers are clearing the road to Taranta, supply by wheeled transport becomes a serious problem and as 2i/c of the Squadron, this task falls on Valerian.

Here, in Palena, another woman makes an entrance: she is known as Maria 'the Peach' (*La Penceija*), Rattelli, *na Diavere* ('a wise woman' in Abruzzan dialect). She is a somewhat ambiguous figure. One testimony, from Antonio Torelli, claims she wore collaborator armbands, perhaps for her earlier behaviour before the Allies arrive. Yet when they do, she demonstrates guile and courage more than once. With her 'generous, sensitive, passionate, courageous, outgoing, unpredictable, mysterious nature' – according to the Italian source – it is said she even has 'paranormal powers'.

She crosses the front line with two others, with no fear of being shot, and rushes to the English command centre in Casoli. 'The whole of

Palena has been mined, everything!' she tells them, and explains how Germans have been given the order that the last one to leave town has the task of blowing it up. She claims she knows how to 'save' the undamaged part of the town. Forced Italian labour has brought explosives and wires into the houses where experts have connected them with fuse wire. Taken to Palena, she advises where the timer is, so the dynamite charges can be defused.

The truth of all this is moot; none of the diaries or interviews mention it. However, Douro reports, she does prove extremely helpful. 'A few days after we arrived a woman appeared from the ruins – out of the mist, as if by magic. She told us that her name is Maria, and asks if we would feed her. She would look after us – wash our clothes and cook for us. She was like an angel of mercy.' She then supplies him with the little black stallion he uses in maintaining supplies to his squadron.

> I used to go down about every second or third night and meet the convoy of mules. Luckily there was a great gorge with a stream, very steep ... It came under the mountain – we couldn't do it in daylight. It was so steep we had to wait till it grew dark and wait for that, bring in the mules and get them out before light. The first time this happened I realised I would want a horse. Maria, through her contacts, obtained a little black stallion, so I went down – he was entire stallion – down the path to the next village ... Of course I didn't realise mules come on heat, and my stallion kept trying to mount all these wretched mules.
>
> Every few minutes I would come under shellfire. Once I had half an hour on my own and I went into houses and found two women in bed, dead. Very eerie. I couldn't do anything. As for the second one, a dog had got into the house, and they are all starving, so the body was pretty well all torn to pieces – it was horrible.

Maria the Peach died in 1980, so Douro was unable to thank her in person when he visited Palena later with his wife and daughter.

The patrolling out of Palena is ceaseless. Fraser is ordered to Palena Station and finds it held by the enemy. Another patrol under Lt Revertera is sent up the mountain where they contact one enemy patrol of six men. Another led by Lt Domvile of B Squadron locates a further enemy position. The enemy is reported to be exceedingly well disciplined and has obviously been prepared for a patrol to try and contact them, as in a very few minutes and with practically no orders as far as could be ascertained, the German patrol set off down the hill in an attempt to cut off Domvile's patrol.

Domvile opens fire and one man is seen to fall. They are highly trained mountaineers and according to the WO Diary, 'move much faster over the ground than our own men, it being the latter's first experience of snow-covered mountain country. Our patrol, however, withdrew without loss.' Clouds come down, and further patrolling is impossible. 'Lessons learnt are that patrols must be properly equipped with mountain equipment, as normal boots and clothing are useless in this type of country, also, teams should be specially trained for this type of patrol.' On this matter du Plessis provides a laconic overview:

After Alamein we were pulled back and sent to the north of Syria with appalling equipment and we were slowly rearmed – and then almost a year later we were re-assembled near Alexandria with a lot more training and lovely new equipment. There we were pushed off to Italy, and in Italy our equipment was useless because all the Germans needed to do was to blow up the roads and bridges and keep an eye from above. So Ian [Van Ammel] and all of us were sent with personal wear which hadn't changed since the desert to do patrols at 3000 feet slipping about in impossible boots. The Colonel put in an urgent emergency request and the Colonel got us climbing boots, socks, warm pullovers and a marvellous thing called a string vest. I don't know why, you can't find it any more. It keeps the shirt off your skin so there's a warm current of air and it acts as a thermos, and you can be almost too hot in it. We were given those, and a woollen bonnet!

Douro records a particular daring act of one of the young officers, with his Corporal of Horse:

We occupied Palena with three forward defensive positions to the North of the town. Palena was a sort of crossroads and a river. There we stayed. We mainly reported on enemy movements, once or twice we sent out patrols. Laurence Rook, who became incidentally a great horseman, for he was in the first Olympics team after the war – Laurence took out a patrol as we were annoyed by an enemy OP fairly close. Laurence got as close as he could and went forward through a minefield with Corp Halls in front giving early warning and shuffling his feet so he didn't tread on mines. Then at pistol point he took prisoner a German Warrant Officer with maps, brought him through the minefield and back. He got an immediate MC for that. Apart from that we sat there – observing, sending out patrols.

John Ewart is having a rather desultory time. His troop is defending the monastery, well away from everyone else, and he feels his men are very inexperienced. He feels lonely, having left the monastery on a patrol on the night of May 11/12,

> ... just by myself with two guerrillas. It seemed to me a bloody job and the interpreter made it sound pretty bad. However there was nothing I could do and prepared for the worst. I left and spent the night wandering about in the dark. Never actually got to the place I was meant to go as guerrillas were given the wrong instructions. It was an anti-climax, all so different to what I expected. We were hardly ever careful and the whole thing was largely a matter of luck. Almost got lost on the way back, on arrival shot at by British Bren gun. Went to bed almost straight away then wrote out report and slept again in afternoon. Reorganised our defences in evening.

It is all very cat and mouse, and for the time being inconclusive for John: 'Tonight Teddy was going out and hoped to ambush a German patrol. At last moment this was changed as they are expecting an attack. More anxiety for me but our little post was considerably strengthened tonight by the addition of the wire. No one got to bed.'

Van Ammel says of the wire: 'We had a whole lot of wire, and a whole lot of cattle bells. We strung the wire out in front of our position so if they came in front of our position the bells would give them away. Halfway through the night the bells started going off like hell. We had set up a couple of Bren guns to do crossfire and we fired. Dead silence. In the morning we found about 12 dead sheep. I shouldn't laugh!'

When, like Ewart, they patrol at night they climb to pre-arranged spot heights on the map, and then observe all the next day before returning the next night to the base. Ever on the alert, they are soon very tired. The Germans, ready for any opportunity to retaliate, mount a small attack, which they repulse.

At 7pm on Thursday May 11 they hear from Murray-Smith, who has been told by Colonel Gooch that the 'big push' is due. 2000 guns between Monte Cassino and the sea are due to open up at 11pm.

CHAPTER SEVEN

A MINIATURE STALINGRAD

My illustrious Army Group Commander, [Montgomery], after giving me my MC ribbon, stepped back and said crisply: 'Patrolling is bloody, isn't it?' When I stammered that it seemed a bit hard that it was always the same people chosen for patrols, he replied with a twinkle in his eye: 'One day you'll command a battalion and you will understand the problem.'

Sydney Jary, *18 Platoon*

New material on Cassino, never before published in English and mainly from Italian sources, has come to light. It is from this that my brief account is sourced, as it provides a stark contrast to the Regiment's stalemate 100 kilometres to the north east, and is to effect what happens to them.

The Allied strategic idea is that Rome, after the Salerno landings, should be 'in the bag' by Christmas 1943. Even with the hesitation and mismanagement of the Italian capitulation and the rapid German invasion, the Allied generals believed the Nazi armies were demoralised and ready to quit. The tide does turn almost straightaway from Salerno onwards, yet directed by Kesselring, who many believe was Hitler's best general, the subsequent defence of Italy is to become arguably the best-fought German campaign of the war.

The Allied advance is slow and in the winter of blizzards, rain and storms raking down from the North and East Abruzzi mountains, they do not arrive until January on the road to Monte Cassino and the

Gustav Line. Ferociously fortified by flood-waters, mines, steel pill boxes, levelled fields of fire through streets and buildings or dug-outs, the Germans bring a new kind of brutal warfare from Stalingrad to Italy: concentrated, as Antony Beevor sees it, 'in the ruins of civilian life. Only now the contestants are reversed, with the Germans becoming the defending Russians.'

There is a four-month deadlock. Churchill and his fellow leaders ignore the reality that the superior forces at their command should dig in and wait for spring. They cling to the mistaken principle that even a battle of attrition is better than standing by and watching the Russians fight. How did this delusion come about, and from where did it continue to draw its power?

Some might say primarily from Rome, and the emotional and psychological need of capturing it from the Germans. In the wider war Rome has no strategic significance, but its symbolic importance, especially to those many British officers and politicians with an education in the classics, and to the Americans, also grounded in the Anglo-Saxon tradition, is paramount. It *has* to be taken. It is a question, as much as anything else, of honour. It needs redemption. As Byron put it:

> While stands the Coliseum, Rome shall stand;
> When falls the Coliseum, Rome shall fall;
> And when Rome falls – the World.

***

The huge scale of the four battles over Monte Cassino would have, in any other century but the 20th, decided the outcome of a war, or brought about regime change or revolution. They have been the subject of many books and much controversy, as well as recrimination, and they brought on the Allied side a return to the casualty rates of the First World War; and although they led to freeing Rome, they did not result in German defeat, only withdrawal.

Capture of the medieval Benedictine Abbey of Monte Cassino, of huge spiritual significance to the Christian world, was the objective. It was, like so many military aims dictated by politicians, a squandering of human life, a scandal. Its Abbot Diamare said, 'One day the whole world will know the true story of what happened at Monte Cassino.'

So can the true story of the Abbey's pivotal importance in the battle and the German defence ever be known? To both sides it presented dilemmas. For the Allies, to shell or not to shell? To bomb or not to bomb? From the Axis side, to fortify and occupy, to use for observation; to defend or to abandon? The feeling voiced in the Allied ranks was 'Catholic boys are dying because we are leaving it alone.'

The monks who lived and worshipped there were 'full of pain and bitterness, impotent witnesses of the gradual destruction of the Abbey'. Their diaries ask why the Allies, fighting to save civilization, were venting their fury on this holy place, in which there is no military objective whatever. On the other hand, if the Germans are really fighting to save civilization, as they claim, why do they not renounce their position on this mountain? Throughout the battle most of the monks and the civilian refugees in the monastery never leave.

Yet for an American mortar commander, Cassino symbolises so much that the Allies are fighting for, 'At the very least it stood for a belief in human dignity and individual worth.' But 'when a choice is to be made between a museum piece and the lives of young men, there is no need for long debate.'

The monastery becomes for them the source of monumental misery. Its bombardment is limited at first, but it becomes greater and greater, and the thousand or more civilians inside are more perilously exposed:

> As the roof and windows were progressively blown in, any sense that the building was safe was lost and it became icy cold and, in rooms where the holes were blocked with sacking or boards, murkily dark. Small wonder that the monks did their best to keep further refugees out, hoping that they would find shelter in caves and outbuildings, or walk north. Small wonder that on occasion they relented and the problem grew worse. During its last days the monastery was an enormous camp, with people sleeping in corridors and stairwells, many deep underground, kept inside for fear of shells. And, literally above all, there was noise; noise that was felt as well as heard; noise loud and continuous that was felt as well as heard; noise loud and continuous, enough to drive people mad.
>
> Tom Aitken, *Cassino*

Amid the bickering, the confused plans of the New Zealand generals Francis Tuker and Bernard Freyburg, the American Mark Clark and the British Field Marshal Alexander, the decision moves ineluctably towards the following.

> Italian friends,
> ATTENTION!
> Until now we have tried in every way to avoid bombarding the monastery of Monte Cassino. The Germans have known how to take advantage of this. But now the fighting is closing still more tightly around the Sacred Precinct. The time has come when we are reluctantly forced to aim our weapons at the monastery itself. We are warning you so that you will be able to save yourselves. Our warning is urgent: Leave the monastery. Go at once. Act on this warning. It has been given for your benefit.
> THE FIFTH ARMY

This leaflet arrives nineteen hours and twenty-eight minutes before the first bomb falls. No temporary truce is worked out to enable those inside to leave. It suits Goebbels and the propagandists that the refugees shall perish so the Germans, who are not inside and behind a 'safe' zone, surround the abbey with machine guns pointing inwards and stop them. So both belligerents have set up an atrocity, intent on foisting blame on the other. A British artillery man later confesses:

> Monte Cassino was an objective hated by every Allied soldier anywhere near it. So when we saw 250 Flying Fortresses buzzing up from the south on that perfectly clear February day, we thought wouldn't it be marvellous if they dropped the whole lot on the monastery, then whoosh, down came 500 tons. There was a colossal cheer, you could have heard it all the way to Naples ... All except this one very close friend of mine, who said, 'What are you thinking of, Douglas? Are we in this war to destroy monasteries?' And then I had a huge double take. I thought, My God, what are we up to? I saw that in the last year and a half we had become literally barbarised. We had become indistinguishable from any other army, the German army, the Russian army, the army of Genghis Khan, part of the great marauding horde whose instinct is to destroy, whose training is to destroy ... A bird of sanity perched on my shoulder. I think he's been there ever since.
>
> Quoted in Rick Atkinson, *The Day of Battle*

Lt John Ewart.

Lt Lord Porchester (Porchey).

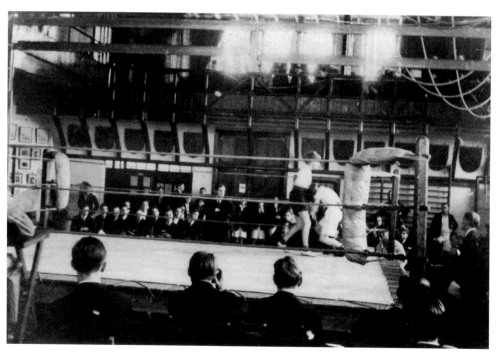

Porchey floored in the Eton-Harrow boxing match.

Capt Marquess Duro.

Lt Gavin Astor.

Maj Tony Murray-Smith.

Capt Neil Foster.

Lt Earl of Uxbridge.

Lt Ian Van Ammel.

Left to Right: Lt John Ewart, Lt Herbert du Plessis, Lt Malcolm Fraser.

Off duty at Sidi Bishr, Lt Van Ammel.

SS *The Empress of Britain.*

SS *Strathnaver* docks at Port Said, 1944.

Allied ships ablaze in Bari harbour, December 1943.

The central piazza at Palena, c. 1900 (above) and St Antony's (below).

St Antony's tower, 1944 (above), and general view of the devastation (below).

Palena rubble, 1944.

A German cartoon mocking the speed of the Allied advance.

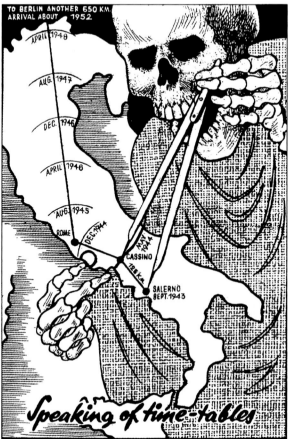

Via San Falco, Palena, 1944.

Polish armour, 5.5in artillery, en route to Monte Cassino.

To all Prisoners of War!

The escape from prison camps is no longer a sport!

Germany has always kept to the Hague Convention and only punished recaptured prisoners of war with minor disciplinary punishment.

Germany will still maintain these principles of international law.

But England has besides fighting at the front in an honest manner instituted an illegal warfare in non combat zones in the form of gangster commandos, terror bandits and sabotage troops even up to the frontiers of Germany.

They say in a captured secret and confidential English military pamphlet,

THE HANDBOOK
OF MODERN IRREGULAR
WARFARE:

". . . the days when we could practise the rules of sportsmanship are over. For the time being, every soldier must be a potential gangster and must be prepared to adopt their methods whenever necessary."

"The sphere of operations should always include the enemy's own country, any occupied territory, and in certain circumstances, such neutral countries as he is using as a source of supply."

England has with these instructions opened up a non military form of gangster war!

Germany is determined to safeguard her homeland, and especially her war industry and provisional centres for the fighting fronts. Therefore it has become necessary to create strictly forbidden zones, called death zones, in which all unauthorised trespassers will be immediately shot on sight.

Escaping prisoners of war, entering such death zones, will certainly lose their lives. They are therefore in constant danger of being mistaken for enemy agents or sabotage groups.

Urgent warning is given against making future escapes!

In plain English: Stay in the camp where you will be safe! Breaking out of it is now a damned dangerous act.

The chances of preserving your life are almost nil!

All police and military guards have been given the most strict orders to shoot on sight all suspected persons.

Escaping from prison camps has ceased to be a sport!

Nazi warning to Van Ammel not to escape.

ARMOURED CAR REGT. WIRELESS LAYOUT

Regimental radio communications and call signs.

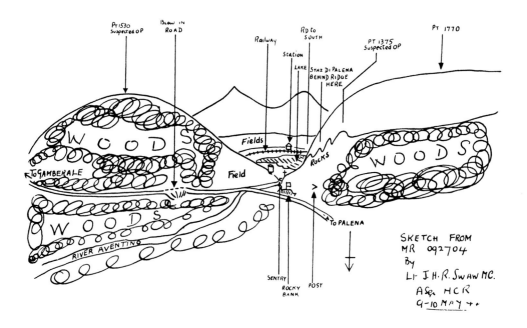

Lt John Shaw's sketch of Palena terrain.

An example of the low-profile Daimler Dingo, ideal for reconnaissance. (From *World War II Trucks and Tanks* by John Norris.)

Trooper Funnel, wireless operator.

Officers of 1HCR with Polish Carpathian Lancers, Colonel Gooch centre right, with Lt-Col Zakrzenski on his right.

The Maiella Mountains.

British troops entering the Temple of Baal, Palmyra.

The Polish Corps insignia, The Maid of Warsaw, which 1HCR men were invited to wear by the Poles in recognition of their contribution, which they did.

The Germans capitalize on the destruction, and get pro-fascist Italians to attest that no German soldiers were in the Abbey. Kesselring announces after the bombing the Abbey is now to be taken into German occupation, and that he will evacuate the monks, nuns and surviving refugees and a truce, requested by Pope Pius XII directly of Hitler, would enable this. But it does not happen. After a brief quiet spell, in which a small trail of refugees and injured leave, the German occupation begins in earnest.

The body of Cardinal Bertolini is dragged out of its tomb, he is divested of his pectoral cross and ring and stuffed into a garden tub. On a wall of a room the monks had used as a refuge and uncovered after its fall, an expert cartoonist draws a tin-hatted Churchill, puffing on a huge cigar and dragging a clutch of toy bombers on strings, gazing disconsolately up at Cassino's ruins from the plain below. A paratrooper ensconced in those ruins jeers, 'Think about it!' A wall painting shows a river, captioned, 'On the lovely banks of the Rhine'.

Ecclesiastical vestments are donned as fancy dress by Germans during a drunken all-night feast. As had happened hundreds of years before, prostitutes ply their trade within the sacred precincts. Troops scavenge among the ruins and pillage the parts left undamaged – as the Nazis condemn the Allies' 'sacrilegious lust for destruction'.

Conveniently prepared for them by the bombing, elite paratroopers, under the overall command of Lt General Fridolin von Senger und Efferlin, a former Oxford Rhodes scholar, make an impregnable fortress of the ruins. This transforms Monte Cassino into what the Allied command had mistakenly supposed it already was: a defensive bastion and observation post, an ammunition dump, and the centre of a complex network of communications.

On February 18, one battle to take Cassino founders. It is followed in March by the battle for Cassino town, from which its 25,000 inhabitants have fled. Intense bombardment from air and artillery again make so much rubble and craters the town furnishes excellent defensive positions for von Senger. He can only wonder at the crass strategy of bombing and the avoidance, even neglect, of orthodox doctrines of street fighting with tanks and infantry. Tanks cannot get in because they are blocked by piles of rubble.

Hitler calls this a battle of the First World War fought with weapons of the Second; Churchill talks of 'a miniature Stalingrad', while the historian Dan Davin calls it 'quite a different kettle of sharks from the usual set battle and much more a deadly game of hide-and-seek'.

> During the eight days it lasted and long afterwards, rats throve on the corpses of men and mules lying in the mud and rubble or floated on the scummy surface of rain-filled bomb craters. The air was rank with the stink of explosives, broken sewers and the vomit-sweet stench of death.
>
> Tom Aitken

As the vicious fighting intensifies, with the advancing New Zealanders bogged down in heavy rain and clinging mud, very few prisoners are taken, and Red Cross flags and armbands ignored. Ralph Trevelyan in *Rome '44* writes:

> Entering Cassino was a vision of the end of the world, past description. It was like some ghastly warning. Would this then be the fate of Rome, or for that matter Paris, or London, or even Auckland? Marching into those ruins brought out a kind of sadism in us. We were really enraged when the Jerries hit back – they had no right even to be *alive*. They were behaving like machines. Some bugger near to me was hit, and he went screaming straight towards the Jerries, not in pain but in sheer fury, like some frantic wild animal scrabbling through the ruins which were covered with a sort of white marble dust – and, God, did that dust dry up your throat. Of course they got him. I can only describe Cassino as looking as if it had been raked over by some monster comb and then pounded all over the place by a giant hammer. There were these vast craters, you see, which when the rain came that night, filled up like lakes, deep enough to drown a wounded man.

Cassino falls, but there is still the mountain of Cassino to conquer. Successive attempts fail. The strongpoints below the Abbey and the heights beyond remain in German hands: by the end of March the Indian assaults on the mountain and the New Zealand advance in the town reach deadlock, and Alexander calls a halt on March 23. Territorial superiority still lies with Kesselring's forces. The Allies have captured the castle, the railway station, most of the town but two embattled hotels on one route (6) 'now sprawling cairns of stone and brick', harbour paratroopers and are now if anything more dangerous to approach. The Germans have even repaired roads and brought forward Mark IV tanks and anti-tank guns to face the infantry attacks.

They do not adhere to the Wellington philosophy of war, for they exult over their triumphant defence. General Veitinghoff tells Kesselring on 25 March that 'no troops but 1 Parachute Division could have held Cassino,' unaware he is parroting Alexander, who on the 22nd writes to Brooke: 'Unfortunately we are fighting the best soldiers in the world – what men! ... I do not think any other troops could have stood up to it perhaps except these para boys.' But while the German defence remains intact, they are in no position to counter-attack. The Allies consolidate and prepare the next bloody expenditure of men.

Von Senger reports: 'The second battle of Cassino has ended in our favour,' but he cautions 'the enemy will probably launch another major attack in the corps sector very soon. He will hardly lie down under his two defeats, as they represent a loss of prestige for him, and have an undoubted effect upon the morale of his armed forces elsewhere and on the international political situation. There is no indication just yet where the enemy plans to strike next.'

Because this profligate Italian campaign has now lasted seven months, Churchill turns testily on Alexander:

> I wish you would explain to me why this passage by Cassino, Monastery Hill, etc., all on a front of two or three miles, is the only place you must keep butting at. About five or six divisions have been worn out going into these jaws. Of course I do not know the ground or the battle conditions, but, looking at it from afar, it is puzzling why, if the enemy can be held and dominated at this point, no attacks can be made on the flanks. It seems very hard to understand why this most strongly defended point is the only passage forward ... I have the greatest confidence in you and will back you up through thick and thin, but do try to explain to me why no flanking movements can be made.
>
> Churchill, *Closing the Ring*

There is an answer.

CHAPTER EIGHT

THE BITTER MOUNTAIN

Discipline and regimental pride are supports but, in decisive moments of great danger, the grip of the leader on the led is paramount. Infantry section and platoon commanders must possess the minds and hearts of their soldiers ... Sound leadership – like true love, to which I suspect it is closely related – is all-powerful.

Sydney Jary, *18 Platoon*

Only 100 kilometres away a completely different set of battle rules apparently apply. The Marquess of Anglesey (then Lieutenant Lord Uxbridge) is stationed at a church when he hears from Captain Henderson, the Adjutant, that the 'great bombardment against Cassino would take place at 11 that evening. We sat there and waited ... and suddenly we were shaken at the great bombardment. Amazing experience but a matter of horror, really.'

Immediately, and not surprisingly, on both sides of the mountains and in the valleys it becomes a much more fierce war zone, and soon the Regiment are to suffer fatalities. The headquarters moves from Lama to the east, closer to Fallascoso, which up to now has been heavily shelled, while at Lama a base is set up of Italian partisans and Regiment officers and men to patrol continuously, observe and harass the Germans. The Germans retaliate with heavier shelling, mortars and machine guns, and an artillery duel develops with the RA Mountain battery, the casualties from which Shaw describes as 'not very good'. By 13.30 the enemy has fired approximately 100 shells on 1HCR positions. Two men are killed and fourteen wounded, while Palena is cut off from supply. Herbert tells us what happens next in A Squadron.

At Palena you could not move by day without risking a shelling from above. We soon learnt that some places, being out of sight, were safer than others. The bridge connecting Palena to the main road had been blown, and supplies delivered to us on one side of the river had to be man-handled about one mile to the village. We thought at first that this section of road was out of sight from the enemy above and that it was safe for the supply operation to be carried out by day. But we were soon to learn how mistaken we were.

At about ten o'clock one morning word came up from the blown bridge that the crossing had been shelled. I was Signals Officer at Squadron Headquarters without much to do, and Murray Smith told me to take a stretcher party down to the river; he was organizing an ambulance to be sent to the blown bridge by Regimental HQ and I was to transfer the casualties to it.

We were just three in the stretcher party: myself, the stretcher party N.C.O. who carried a rolled up Red Cross flag and wore Red Cross arm-bands, and my soldier servant Trooper Freeman. We made our way down the winding road to the blown bridge and in a short while the bend in the road revealed the river. We heard the whistle and crump of mortar bombs and we began to bend at the waist and then to creep on our knees. Eventually we were crawling in the ditch along the side of the road because shrapnel was flying and you needed to be low to be beneath it. A few more yards and the scene before us was clear: where the road curled back on itself behind a spur and the river went forward away from the road there were two men in the water. One lay still and the other was moving his limbs, lying on his back. The river at this point was a fast flowing mountain stream of shallow water splashing over and around low-lying rocks. The two bodies were half submerged.

Our orders were simple: to get those casualties back to the ambulance. But the mortar fire was lethal. We had a decision to make. The Corporal and I consulted each other more by eye contact than by word of mouth. At length I said, 'We wait for a lull?' He was silent for a moment and then he said, 'There's a lull now.' We stood up and went forward down into the water. The Corporal held his Red Cross flag straight up over his head with one hand, one end of the folded stretcher resting on his other hand. We waded in as best we could over the slippery uneven river bed, up to our knees.

The two bodies lay some yards apart. I recognized Trooper Musham first and there was no doubt he was dead. His face was the colour of the grey-green rocks he was lying on. The Corporal stopped, touched his head and said, 'He's dead, Sir. We can't do anything for him.' He turned his whole attention to Trooper Hislop, the next casualty. He had been the driver of my armoured car, now the corners of his mouth were drawn right back to his ears, his strong teeth bared and clenched to stifle the grunts of extreme pain.

We had crossed the threshold of fear and left it behind when we stood up and waded into the water. We knew that our chances of survival were exactly fifty-fifty: either Jerry would respect our Red Cross flag and let us in; or he would ignore it and we were done for. This was the killing place and his mortar was accurately ranged on it.

But on this occasion it seemed that the Germans were being perfect gentlemen. Our whole attention now was on our rescue operation; we were giving it the time it needed. I knelt down in the water and held the stretcher steady against the current which was trying to tear it away. The two stretcher men lifted Hislop and placed him on the stretcher. Hislop was the Regimental heavyweight boxing champion and he must have weighed fifteen stone plus. They raised their heavy burden and began their stumbling journey to the shore. The river bed was slippery and uneven. The Corporal led the way and I gave a hand at the rear of the stretcher. When we reached the shore I let them go on to the bend in the road where the ambulance was waiting, safe and out of sight.

An idea came to me that I might be able to haul Musham out of the water by myself. He was a very big heavy man like Hislop but I felt sure I could haul him out by the shoulders. I went back and knelt down under his shoulder to lift and haul; but the most unexpected thing then happened: the noise which came from his body was like broken crockery in a sack. He must have taken the full blast of a mortar bomb and been terribly cut up inside. I had the horrible feeling that if I pulled hard enough he might come apart.

As I was about to give up the whole idea of pulling Musham clear the whistle and crump of a bomb came from just down river. This was Jerry saying he had given us enough time. I didn't need further persuasion.

With one bound, as they say, (or perhaps two or three!) I was out of there, flattening myself into the scrub on the river side. A lull, several more bounds and I had caught up with the stretcher which had just reached the ambulance. 'His leg is bad,' I said superfluously to the medical orderly but he was already squeezing a morphine tablet into Hislop's mouth.

I can't remember much about our journey back up the hill except that I saw a detachment of unknown troops, they may have been sappers, dug into a deep ditch between the road and the hillside. They had had a ringside view and they would have been there from the very beginning: perhaps about one hour? No one apparently had felt inclined to go in and help Hislop.

Back at Squadron Headquarters in Palena I went to report to Tony and Valerian who were bursting for news. 'There were two casualties only,' I said. 'Hislop and Musham. Musham was dead. We got Hislop into the ambulance all right.' What did you do with Musham? 'We left him there, in the water.'

Tony's face darkened. He took a few steps here and there across the room. 'We can't have that, leaving a body there in the sun.' I was appalled. It seemed that I had messed up. I was waiting to be told to go back and get him out; or worse still, to suffer the indignity of having someone else go down and do the job that I hadn't done correctly. After a while Tony said: 'You had better go and put some dry clothes on.'

I slunk away, miserable. I was icy cold and wanted to be sick. I began to shake and couldn't control it. I found the ruck sack beside my bedroll and fished out some clean underpants, a dry pair of khaki trousers, a clean pair of socks. It was a brilliant spring day but I pulled on a jersey. After a while I regained control and went back to Squadron H.Q.

Tony was on the field telephone to Headquarters and his face had recovered its sardonic good humour. I remember the phrase 'They nearly killed Herbert!' He was looking at me not unkindly and I knew this was a signal of forgiveness. I was back from being an outcast. 'We'll recover Musham after dark,' he said.

It took me a long time to forget the sight of Hislop's teeth grinding in agony, and the sound of Musham's shoulders on my chest making those broken noises when I lifted. In fact, I haven't forgotten.

***

103

The breakthrough at Cassino triggers more chilling and gruesome episodes. Kenneth Diacre, Van Ammel's future brother-in-law, is sent on a probing patrol. Meantime (and far too late in the day) eight US officers and sergeants with Swiss or German names are transferred to coach the Regiment in mountain warfare – one, a Swiss, had defected from a German mountain regiment.

A five-man patrol (Lt Coats, Trooper Allen, a wireless operator and two partisans) sets out at midnight to climb Monte Amaro the rest of the night, and be in position by first light to observe. They have no climbing instruction, nor mountain boots. The night is very dark, and for most of the time they traverse thick woods.

Coats has put his faith in his Italian guides, who, he has been assured, know the way perfectly. The slopes grow steeper and steeper and are covered in loose stones, so it is very slow going. About 3 am the guides halt and listen. Stones begin rolling down from above, and they hear faint voices from a German patrol.

Just as it starts to get light the patrol emerges from woodland on to a bare hillside. They scramble to the summit and find they are on a razor-backed ridge; the ideal observation post.

The Italians suddenly shout '*Tedeschi, Tedeschi*' and flee. Coats, confused, then sees five Germans advancing along the ridge towards him. Trooper Allen spots another patrol skirting the foot of the mountain. Coats decides to withdraw. Just below their position is a 'scree' run covered with snow, and they proceed to slide down. Coats can't stop when he hits the end of the snow, and goes on sliding over stones. He gets up as quickly as he can but by the time he stops his hands are cut and the back part of his battledress trousers is no more: gone, too, is a considerable amount of his anatomy. Trooper Allen is unhurt.

Two figures emerge from the woods – the Italian guides who had shot off so quickly knowing capture would mean death. It took the patrol seven hours to climb the Monte Amaro, and forty minutes to come down. A narrow escape, but Coats is out of action. Incredible as it seems, even by this time no one is aware that 'Tedeschi' is Italian for 'German'.

Next night A Squadron is on standby expecting a German counter-attack – especially in the very early morning. To suffer and withstand sitting around being shelled, even if often inaccurately shelled, is not a happy experience. Morale soared when one advanced and went into a fighting patrol! Fraser:

Had little sleep on account of double sentries, even in the house. Went to sleep again, after stand to for a couple of hours. After breakfast, took Cpl Gatlands setting up to fill sandbags and finish working in positions – our 4.2″ mortars opened up again at 10.00 until 11.30 on some Germans seen up in the mountains: good shooting, but negative results.

After lunch, wrote up diary – we are being relieved tomorrow night by C squadron who are forward, but not actively engaged. Just about time too I think. Rations very short although the men don't complain. One sardine, 2 or 3 biscuits and a mug of tea is not enough for me for lunch, when the cupboard is full of food! But Cpl H may be justified. He is doing the feeding arrangements. Go round all sections posts at 7.00pm. Am sleeping up in Tp HQ again. Message comes through on the telephone about 11.30pm from Tony saying 'D' force has sent a signal saying Enemy attack very likely at dawn tomorrow. Two flares sent up by us during the night and one grenade thrown by 7th Tp, but no definite movements. Night dry but cold. Ian Van Ammel and Cpl Halls on patrol (36 hrs) with 1OR [other rank] plus wireless set and two partisans.

The intense activity continues unabated. They think Italian civilians seen in front of Amaro are Germans in disguise. Thirty-four mortar shells fall on Palena by evening. They arrest an Italian who has dug an arrow which points to their machine gun position: they believe he is the cause of the mortar fire.

Germans, some on skis, are reported at various locations. One patrol passes within ten yards of the enemy. More are wounded from shellfire. In the excitement death and injury become an abstraction. Ewart notes the tidying up and that too many rations are left over (a case of hoarding by cooks and quartermaster mismanagement). It is hardly, he writes, worth him going to sleep. He reads a bad book. He mentions seeing German sentries, but not being fired on, nor does he mention the death of the Corporal. He notes that one officer (Lt Teddy Lambton) complains the Squadron 'stinks' and wants to leave, that someone gets drunk and beats up some Italians, that he gets a rocket from his Squadron Leader for not making a full enough report. Fraser reports how 'lucky' they are to have only two casualties.

After two weeks in the very exposed position in Palena, A Squadron withdraws to Toricella. As it leaves, Van Ammel and his Corporal of

Horse, Halls, have been out on patrol for a day and a half and not come back. One officer is worried. Ewart:

> Bed and hour's sleep till 8.30. After an inspection of kit, Tony gave a talk to the squadron in which he said that everyone had done very well. Didn't consider his speech was as good as usual but he does not look at all well and has not had a sleep for some time. Slept in the afternoon. We withdrew to a place called Toricella (Peligna). We have a mess there and the troops are all in billets. In evening after dinner finished organizing my things and went to bed at 12. Yesterday Ian Van Ammel and CoH Halls did not come back from patrol. We all hope that they are both prisoners and not hurt. It just shows you how important luck is – you could not have had a better officer and N.C.O. We are all very sorry that we hardly realised it in the rush of everything.

The Regimental Diary records starkly:

> 5 Germans seen approx. 1600 hrs, 2 halted and 3 started to work round fl. Machine Pistol started firing from rear of Lieut. Van Ammel's posn at 100yds range. Guerrilla withdrew, nothing further heard of Lieut. Van Ammel or CofH. Halls. Patrol sent out to try to find any trace of the missing personnel. NTR. Posted missing.

CHAPTER NINE

THE FORTUNES OF WAR

If the enemy is an ass and fool and prating coxcomb, is it meet, think you, we should also be, be an ass and a fool and a prating coxcomb? In your own conscience now?

Fluellen, *Henry V*

Van Ammel and his patrol had moved down early on May 16 to observe the mortar positions. They found their WT set did not work and Ian sent the partisan plus the wireless operator back to H.Q.

I had Corporal of Horse Halls and two partisans. Neither spoke English. I didn't speak Italian. All sorts of sign language and rather dark. I noticed when we were clambering up during the night in mist and fog and it got light that one of the partisans was shaking like a leaf. I thought it must be the cold. We couldn't make this bloody wireless work so I sent it back. Herbert tells one they'd changed the net – they could hear me but I couldn't hear them. We came below the mist and saw a couple of Germans who were on their bellies with binoculars looking down at Palena. There was no firing. They were on top of a gully which went all the way down the side of a mountain. We stayed very quiet for ten minutes and saw no one. We decided to take them prisoner, but the partisans refused to agree to this, and made off up the mountain again. We were just about to crawl out the gully when about ten men, heavily armed, on skis, pop up and say, '*Komm mit uns.*'

Herbert explains the primitive nature of communications:

> We had a wireline to HQ on the other side of the river Aventino. Normally
> we had normal communication. It was quite a business, the generator
> had to recharge batteries which were huge and took about six gallons of
> petrol – all you could do is to carry a couple of days and somehow I don't
> remember Tony talking to HQ on wire. For the patrols on foot you had a
> little wireless set. I dealt with these when they came out brand-new, and
> Ian, when he was captured, unfortunately had a dud one. At that time
> of the war you had to test all equipment in order to be sure it worked,
> because it was being made in England by people who are not profession-
> als. I was lucky in one respect, I had a marvellous sergeant from REME.
> He would test all of this, run the set until it developed a fault, and then
> remedy it – the only way you knew it was reliable.

One reliable factor common to all war is the unreliability of equipment;
another is a large casualty count from friendly fire, or stepping on your
own mines. So Van Ammel was 'about to capture the two observers but
damn me! – "Hinderhof! Put up your hands!"'– they were surprised and
taken on Monte Amaro 'by an inquisitive bunch of "superior"Austrian
mountain troops on skis'. They are 'in the bag' – another hunting, or
rather shooting, term.

> They were very curious ... Thank goodness they were Austrian. They took
> our Tommy guns and grenades, and one of them started pulling out the
> pin of a Mills bomb. I was in a terrible dilemma. 'Should I stop that? Or
> what?' – I decided discretion was the better part of valour. They are all
> peering down, it would have blown the lot of them sky high – me as well
> ... I stopped him. Otherwise you'd have become a suicide bomber – I don't
> think that was my role.

This is the story of POW No. 1302 G8/VII 4, taken prisoner May 16,
1944, at 1430 hrs. He is twenty-two years old. Austrians have disarmed
him and his Corporal of Horse of their Tommy guns and grenades. The
moment when one started to pull the ring of the grenade has passed.

> I was taken back to their company HQ in the mountains. A little house
> of some sort, a hovel. I was locked in a cupboard, myself and Corporal

Halls. The partisans ahead of us took off up the mountains when they saw us captured, and had escaped. The next day I went to a civilian jail in Sulmona – they had a bloody great visitors' book, probably still there! I had to sign it! I was eventually let out into a courtyard with a rag-tag bunch of criminals – the Italians had emptied the prisons when they opted out of the war, and the Germans were locking them up again. Most of the prisoners were in civilian clothes by this time including Wally Hogg and Pitts [other captured officers]. I told them my name, and suddenly one of them said, 'I know your brother, he's in the Buffs.' Well it's a small world.

It's true my brother was with the Buffs when they invaded West Africa and they fought in Tunisia, Sicily, up the Adriatic side. They were a well known division – the Battleaxe Division due to their insignia. My brother, strangely named Adolph, was a temporary infantry major in 5th Battalion The Buffs, and later was decorated with the D.S.O.

I said to them, You know who I am but I don't know who you are, but let the Germans know because I am wary of them because of my Dutch name, so I could be mistaken for a South African commando. Hitler had issued his orders that caught commandos were to be shot, and we knew of commando operations which had been launched, and nothing further was heard of the men. It wasn't just rumour.

I was interrogated for days. One night I was hauled out of bed at 1.30am. There was a dark room with a table, and a light which shone onto the table into my eyes. Suddenly there was a rattle of machine gun fire. 'That is what we do to people who will not talk.' So why are they doing this? Losing the war, waiting for the inevitable orders to withdraw? I almost laughed. There was a huge German wearing a leather overcoat. They thought I knew more of the intentions of the Regiment than I did. After the war we learnt that a raiding commando party, all Canadians, who landed at La Spezia, had been betrayed by fascists, then caught and shot. Would this be my fate?

***

With Trooper Musham dead and Van Ammel and his Corporal of Horse Halls missing presumed dead or prisoners, the whole complexion of this campaign changes. Shelling, mortaring, bombing, the hazards of crossing a minefield blow away the illusion that you can be safe from death. You are sitting there, you are moving around, and some completely random projectile makes no allowance for how heroic or good a soldier you may be. An artillery barrage, a release of guided missiles, is completely impersonal and in some ways to be pressing buttons to cause the death of unseen people is as impersonal and cold-blooded an exercise as mass slaughter by poisonous gas or flooding a village. (The Nazis flooded thousands of acres of Pontine marshes reclaimed painstakingly by Italian farmers.) In primitive warfare there was skill in defence and attack, but avoiding or escaping death or injury in modern warfare is more a matter of luck. As Marlantes expresses it:

> Understanding that combat will be a dark and terrible initiation *before* one goes into combat will help provide some structure and meaning to this soul-battering experience. A large part of treating PTSD [Post Traumatic Stress Disorder] is simply getting the veteran to remember and talk about what happened to him. The more psychic structure or framing that is brought to the experience of combat, the easier it will be to cope with the experience afterward. It can help provide a bit of meaning in an often meaningless situation. As it is, young warriors' minds and souls are going to be battered and overwhelmed. Killing someone *will* affect you. Part of you *will* think you've done something wrong. It's drilled in from babyhood. If, however, you're prepared ahead of time for it, you'll suffer less because of this.
>
> *What it is like to go to war*

The disappearance of Van Ammel is a significant event as managing, surviving, succeeding in these patrols is the special skill of the Regiment. Everyone notices Ian is gone. It's the first thing, almost, in 2012 that these veterans in their late eighties remember to tell me: Van Ammel 'went into the bag'.

Yet it hasn't taken long for the Regiment to realise the enemy confronting them on the mountain is a decent enemy: the temporary truce for Herbert and the medical orderly to recover Musham and Corporal Hislop have shown them that respect for fallen comrades existed on both sides.

Four days after Van Ammel's patrol was lost, on May 20, Fraser reports:

May 20. While C Squadron are in Palena – A German deserter walked in this evening. He was a young Bavarian from an 'Ack Ack' section over-looking Palena and has given us some very useful information indeed as regard to their positions, strength, etc. He also added that he thought Ian and Halls were unhurt.

Eleven days later, Porchey writes to his father: 'Poor Ian Van Ammel in the Blues was put in the bag a fortnight ago. I hope he is okay. Germans are not so huge and strong as they are made out to be, in fact I think very hungry. Seems very funny since I was playing bridge with Ian three weeks ago.'

CHAPTER TEN

THE SLAUGHTER CONTINUES — THE WINNING DEFENDERS AT CASSINO

> Although they lost, the German soldiers and their families are proud of their exploits, many of which were considerable. It is, of course, very much in their own interest to encourage the theory and myth that, although superior as fighting men, they were beaten only by numerically superior forces and firepower.
>
> Sydney Jary, *18 Platoon*

The German or Axis forces' weakness in this mountain encounter is their reluctance to patrol at night. The Regiment, its three Squadrons, A, B, and C, patrol extensively day and night, while the enemy avoids doing this. By day they produce a devastating display of firepower. The few references to the little probing attacks they make and get nowhere attests to the thorough infantry efficiency of the Cavalry Regiment. Palena and its approaches are where the Regiment stood its ground; well defended, continually shelled and mortared, only able to be supplied and reinforced by night but never attacked, although the threat was constantly there. So much care had been put into training, stimulating the men's imagination, initiative and their individual resourcefulness to probe, draw conclusions, infiltrate and exploit weakness in the enemy's disposition, that they are now seasoned and experienced in the real thing.

The Germans show, I hope I may say without stereotyping, much greater enthusiasm for boasting. Memory fades quickly and easily becomes misleading, prone to distortion. Stories or exploits told over and over again assume a simplified, florid dimension with detail lost in the need for drama.

One hundred kilometres to the west, by the end of May 1944, the Germans have finally been ousted from Monte Cassino. Yet many Germans consider it a victory. Among the dozens of accounts of the Cassino battles, we find several instances of a curious schoolboy mixture of frankness, a determination to portray the Germans as triumphant whatever happened, and nostalgia for the moment when they were on the winning side.

Before the guns open up on May 11 and the offensive *Diadem* begins, there is in that desolate ruined landscape 'a passive state of sustained awfulness'. Rats have grown fat on the bodies nobody could reach. The stench was colossal. A German pioneer reports that British soldiers caught the rats, loaded them into empty sandbags and when night came chucked them into suspected German observation points. Unlike those of the Regiment, Allied patrols helplessly blundered through minefields, so their comrades heard explosions meaning 'some poor bloke on a patrol had copped it. Sometimes there would be a scream, you've no idea how chilling; I once heard some chap calling desperately, a woman's name, always fainter, as if saying goodbye for eternity before he died this agonizing death.' (R. Trevelyan, *Rome '44*)

German morale remains high and on April 22 Hitler's birthday is enthusiastically celebrated, with Nazi flags decked all over occupied villages. In this period, before the 50,000-strong Second Polish Corps commanded by General Anders began its assault following 11,000 artillery pieces opening up along a 20-mile front, the battle zone was frozen into a 'vast stricken graveyard'. Cassino was no longer news.

The Poles, with reckless determination and courage, and carrying an extra 30 or 40 pounds of grenades each, attacked furiously, attempting to encircle town and Abbey. At first heavily repulsed, with massive loss of life, they attacked again and again, while the British forces crossing the River Rapido west of Cassino advanced up the Liri Valley.

The Polish Corps arrived at Cassino carrying a great deal of emotional baggage. They loathed Germany, their 'hereditary enemy', and its people. Germany's invasion of Poland in 1939 had begun the war; ever since then Poles at home and in exile, had been forced to suffer in impotence what the Gestapo were doing to their homeland. At Cassino they thought principally of killing as many Germans as recklessly as possible, with maximum bravado. They took unnecessary risks and despised the prudent approach of British soldiers who thought of war as a matter of duty rather than glory. Emotional extremes marked Polish response to the battle, the first large-scale confrontation in which, as the Second Polish Corps, they had been involved.

Tom Aitken

The reckless bravado, for which they paid dearly, prevails. The tipping point, which arrives in every battle, is reached on May 17 when, after further attack and counter-attack, the Poles secure the key *Colle San Angelo* and its gorse cover. As General Anders wrote, they are at the moment 'when both sides face each other in a state of complete exhaustion, apparently incapable of making any further effort, and when the one with the stronger will, who is able to deliver the final blow, wins.'

The battle-scarred German paratroopers, fully encircled, withdraw, so at last two Polish soldiers raise their red-and-white national flag and the Union flag over the ruined monastery, which has been defiantly impregnable throughout: 'It did not fall to direct assault, or succumb to the heaviest weapons available to the Allies. Now it was no longer important.'

Welsh Guardsmen, who had valiantly held onto Rocca Janiah, a nearby strongpoint they had captured earlier, cheerfully join the celebration of victory, descending the slope of death. A journalist who investigates a dead man who has served as marker is blown to bits by the booby-trapped corpse.

'When at last [Cassino] town fell and we ventured forth in daylight we found outside the door of the gaol some honeysuckle, a tall flower and a lovely red rose growing in the rubble.' (L.F. Ellis, *The Welsh Guards at War.*)

War pauses, then moves on. In the Household Cavalry microcosm the Germans hold out longer than at Cassino. C Squadron is to invest Palena, while A Squadron is to move out to Toricella. Ewart is not too keen on the move: 'Rather unpleasant moving into a new house in the dark but it has to be done ...' Before he does:

May 16. Stood to at 4.30 this morning as an attack is expected at Palena. I was up on guard at 3.30 so did not get much sleep. All day began clearing up and tidying things ready for C Squadron to take over tonight. Found we had too many rations left over – as usual, a case of hoarding by cooks as well as mismanagement of the Quartermaster's department. My troop has gone to stay at the embassy point tonight till all the troopers have been withdrawn. We had to carry our kit about a mile so we arranged to tie it all on a cart. However this did not work so eventually we carried it. Put the 2 rations in position (twice) and then waited. Halfway through the night [Trooper] Driburgh fired some shots at imaginary enemy – good thing no one was there as we had a very weak defence. Finally last troop withdraw about 4 and arrived back at 5am. Could not find a bed roll but it was hardly worth going to bed so eventually I find it and had an hour's sleep.

The Austrians above set a trap for a patrol led by a US mountain warfare expert. The patrol see a dead German farther up the slope: one man is sent to investigate and roughly thirty of the enemy appear and try to encircle the patrol. The dead German has been put out as bait. They withdraw without casualties. They report that up the mountain at this point there is only one track; that the Germans know it, and watch it carefully; and they will have to find a new route if patrols are to get up the mountain unobserved in future.

Ewart maintains his attendance at mass through thick and thin and we can intuit, as with the others, how his faith punctuates and stabilizes his life.

Woken up by Chandler at 6 and told I had to be ready to go on recce at 7.20. Did not understand at first but certainly it appears that I was going to recce a position for protecting more guns that were coming up. Went with Valerian to KRH and then Colonel said that I was not wanted so went back to Toricella. Read. Then went to Mass and Communion in Gessopalena. Meant to have gone on mortar protection tonight but it was thought unnecessary and I did not have to go thank goodness. In afternoon went to Casoli for bath but both houses are shut so came back and watched Valerian shooting pigeons. In evening after dinner argument with John, Teddy and Valerian about treatment of Italians.

Palena is evacuated, leaving only two troops as a listening post; fearing a night attack, the rest of C Squadron is placed over the Aventino, ready to counter-attack. At first light they reoccupy Palena, as they do not want the enemy to believe they have retreated. It seems, here, that the Regiment's honour is at stake. Plans are made to attack positions west of Palena, but then put on hold, for what would be the point if the enemy were to withdraw anyway?

Mines are a constant hazard. The German anti-personnel *Schu* mine, is particularly tiresome to deal with. A small box with the lid slightly open, it detonates when pressure is put on its lid. It normally blows off an ankle or leg to the knee and causes a number of fatalities, mainly as the result of shock.

The Sappers lay a minefield just outside Palena, and proving perhaps Herbert's point that no-one in the army knows what's happening or if they do they don't tell anyone, the location of the field is unknown. On May 26, Lieutenant Colonel Fenton, CO of the Mountain Artillery Regiment, with his Adjutant and RSM. take a short cut across Palena and walk straight into the minefield, where they are blown up.

Fenton is killed outright, his adjutant and RSM badly wounded. C Squadron Troop Corporal Barrett is sent to rescue them; he too steps on a mine and is killed, followed by two HCR troopers, Capps and Thomas, who, still without knowing where the mines are, bring out the dead and wounded. 'A very brave deed as they were all dead or badly hurt' (Fraser). During this, German mortars open fire. The mountain artillery duel that ensues knocks out three 25 pounders and 5.5 mediums, killing another man and wounding five.

Shaw, rather nonchalantly, refers to the enemy's accuracy 'causing casualties', and calls the minefield disaster a 'mishap'. He sustains the Regiment's convivial mood. May 24 is fairly typical:

> Went to Bomba to buy wine with Valerian. On the way called in on Nick to settle a few things and shot a rat. Got forty litres of fairly good wine in Bomba and met George Murray Smith on the way back. Hoped to see the mortar experts as well but they had moved. Arrived back to find a ration of whisky and gin in, an excellent development.

Deserters from the Nazi ranks, Poles and Yugoslavs, are now pouring in, while escaped or freed Allied POWs from the west or north appear more frequently. One such escapee is Dan, Earl of Ranfurly, ADC to General Neame, who had escaped the previous autumn. Neame, General

O'Connor, Air Marshal Boyd and Ranfurly all spent the winter evading capture as they infiltrated German lines choked with transport, avoiding the roads. 'We were into the High Apennines, and the snow had a hard crust which one stepped through sometimes up to one's thighs.' Ranfurly ultimately made it to the east coast and onto a fishing vessel. He sailed through the night to reach Ortona harbour and safety.

Gavin Astor, the Intelligence Officer, welcomes Tuesday, May 30 as a 'glorious day – as glorious a day as one could wish for'.

> V Corps was holding the northern sector of the line from the Adriatic to the Maiella Mountains with 10th and 4th Indian Divisions. The mountains in the centre of Italy were being patrolled and watched by four cavalry regiments, the HCR, and CIH under 4th Indian division and the KDGs and 12th Royal Lancers under 8th Army. To the left of these and extending up to the Anzio beachhead the Allied line was bitterly fighting its way towards Rome having broken down the defences at Cassino.

On duty that same night of May 30/31, Fraser has a busy time:

> At approximately 4.30pm I heard that a German patrol of 3 men had been seen approaching Palena monastery, our troops opened fire and wounded one of them who fell over into a gully. The other two made off at full speed. A party of 10 partisans was then ordered to go and get them, killing both with TSMG fire and bringing in the bodies and the wounded man as well ...
>
> ... At 11.30pm a 15 cwt ruck left R.HQ with a guard to collect the Germans. By this time 2 more deserters had just walked in so there was a total of 5 to collect, 3 alive and 2 dead. The truck eventually arrived back at 12.30 with everyone, having stopped by a building in Fallascoso, the prisoners were first told to get out. Having got them out and keeping them covered we told them to take out the two dead bodies. These were lying on a piece of board face downwards dressed normally. They did not smell then but they were full of bullet holes and very bloody about the head and neck.

The prisoners rather reluctantly bring out the bodies, which are then dumped on a room on the floor. They are then escorted upstairs to another room with a lantern to await interrogation by the IO. Astor:

In company with Ian Henderson and Leo Arundel our MO I immediately conducted a brief 'tactical squeeze' to gain what information I could before dispatching them to Div. and afterwards inspected the two corpses with RCM Barrett.

The two deserters, one a Pole and the other a Yugoslavian, had been impressed into a German artillery regiment. The PW was from an Alpine Regiment, which had recently arrived in the Palena station from Austria. He had been sent out with a sergeant and another man to find out if Palena village was occupied.

Fraser took a good look at the men in that room:

The first man, the actual prisoner, had a graze on his forehead but was otherwise unwounded. He wore the normal German uniform and peaked cap, but was a surly rascal and a little truculent. He was an Austrian who had not been out of Germany more than three weeks and belonged to an Alpini Regiment, he was not very tall but had a good physique and didn't compare to the two weedy little deserters. This Austrian also wore a badge on his left breast pocket denoting that he was an Olympic Runner. The other, a Pole and a Yugoslavian, were dressed the same and all wore good boots. They were not unduly thin but were nothing compared to the Austrian. We gave them some bully and biscuits which they ate ravenously but said little except mutter a little amongst themselves. I also had a look through their papers and personal effects. The Pole had a very nice wallet full of photographs. Rather good ones too, of his wife, family groups, people skiing etc. There were also other odds and ends and a pay book of course. These two were of a different regiment to the prisoner.

After they have been interrogated and each has given a good deal of information, they are packed off in the truck to Lanciano with their escort.

My troop then came down to the house and between us we carted the two bodies up the hill onto the road again to be collected some hours later. They were an absolute dead weight and were beginning to smell a bit but we managed somehow. I had a good look at them and there literally must have been about a TSMG magazine full in each of them. They were absolutely plastered with bullet holes from the heels down the back to the bottom of the spine. Their shirts were very mucky and they themselves were of course stone cold, white and clammy. Their arms dangled about all over the place. They were dispatched in a lorry about 3am and taken away to be buried – where I do not know and I care less. We were glad to get rid of them.

Gavin Astor has an early breakfast next morning:

> I set off with the Colonel to recce new positions for C Squadron, which was going to take over from the right-hand Squadron of the KDG. We collected Ferris St George, commanding C Squadron on our way through Torricella and, and sent a LO from Corps at the point where the Perano road leaves the River Sangro. He 'painted a picture' of the situation and I quickly copied our own and the KDG's new locations off his map. We were each extending further to the left, so that in our case we could include Palena Station in the area to be patrolled. He told us that the KDG detachment which had been based on Pizzoferrato and Gamberale had 'either moved out last night all would be doing so this morning'. Our own C Squadron would not be moving into these positions until four o'clock in the evening!

These villages are only 8 miles distance from the HQ but it is about 30 miles round by road. Astor takes a jeep with his driver Rossiter and two dispatch riders on bikes follow along the sinuous and dusty roads. He is to meet up with Gooch at a certain crossroads if they get parted. One of the riders has a puncture and they stop to tinker with the tyre, but he fails to mend it, so they leave him behind. On reaching the rendezvous they find Gooch has not waited. So the Astor jeep and one rider push onto Gamberale. They are now in no-man's land, some 8 or 10 miles between the German posts and their own, patrolled by both sides. Gamberale is

> ... an eerie little place labelled with 'Mines', 'Booby traps', 'Keep out' etc. Totally unoccupied except for two old women who were grovelling about in the ruins. We stopped here and looked at the map. There were no signs of the Colonel. It was about one o'clock. Should we stop here and have our lunch or push on the extra two or three miles to Pizzoferrato? I hailed an Italian labourer who happened to be working nearby and asked him if he had seen another jeep like mine, to which he replied 'No'. He told me

that a number of vehicles had left the night before, so I gathered the KDGs had moved out.

Astor decides to push on to Pizzoferato to await Gooch and eat lunch. This is the last the Regiment hears of him. The sudden disappearance of this ubiquitous and popular officer unsettles and perplexes the others. Fraser records:

> We heard at 2am (June 1st) that Gavin Astor's jeep had been found just outside Gamberale a total wreck and burnt to pieces. Pieces of bedding and clothing were found but not a sign of a drop of blood or a body. The jeep we gathered had met with some MG fire from an ambush patrol, swerved into the side and blown up on two mines.

Ewart is woken at 2am and finds it 'all rather a shock', especially as Herbert is now also missing, out on patrol.

With death now a daily occurrence, the Regiment has been in action a month. Ewart, a trainee gunnery officer by now, has been in the army a year – like Porchey. Half the Regiment has been on operations for nearly four years, and although by mid-1944 the majority of the troopers are from a post-1940 intake drafted in from the training regiment at Windsor, there is a remarkable degree of continuity among the officers and non-commissioned officers. They are family.

While Porchester is sent out to recce the area around Astor's burnt-out jeep, du Plessis' patrol returns safe on June 1. Still no word of Astor.

CHAPTER ELEVEN

EPIPHANY — BUT OTHERS DO TIME

The other man did not *draw our attention* to anything, he taught us a different game in place of our own – But how can the new game have made the old one obsolete? – We now see something different and can no longer naively go on playing.

> Ludwig Wittgenstein, *Remarks on the Foundation of Mathematics*

The Allies enter Rome on June 4 and D-Day in Normandy follows two days later, overshadowing it. The expenditure of men and arms to achieve this strategically unnecessary, symbolic victory has possibly been greater than for the whole of the rest of the Western Europe campaign and fall of Germany.

To coincide with the fall of Rome, many explosions in the enemy lines signify withdrawal and the Regiment multiplies its patrols to learn the truth. Once again, death strikes at random.

Trooper Rogers from a C Squadron patrol, bloodstained and hatless, staggers into Squadron HQ to tell how his patrol commander John Roberts, formerly one of Atlee's private secretaries, a married man with two children, and Corporal Price have stepped on a mine and are lying injured at Palena Station. Rogers, who had extraordinary strength, barely survived the mine blast and had walked or crawled 10 miles to safety. A further patrol takes five hours to find Roberts and Price, now dead, and has to leave the bodies unburied, but returns to HQ with maps, documents and personal belongings.

The fortunes of war are now dramatically different. Fraser:

June 8. At about 5.30pm 7 civilians from Campo de Giove [the other side of Monte Amaro] arrive carrying a white flag. All seemed delighted to have arrived. One speaks quite good English. They say that the Germans have left Campo Giove last night, taking with them just about everything that they could lay their hands on, in the way of foods etc, also four guns. This news was also brought to us earlier, by 4 other civilians from there who came over the mount. Thick mist covers down from about 8pm and stays down until early midnight.

A usual early morning 'stand to' etc. Wash and shave after breakfast. Get orders through H.Q. to withdraw forward O.P. at once into building and make road block by crater in road. This completed by lunchtime. Germans now known to be clear of Campo de Giove, which is also un-mined. German P.O.W. found there held by partisans, and sent back report that he was on patrol which captured Ian V.A. and C of H Halls. They were both OK. Afternoon, two wounded Italians arrive who blew themselves up on a mine this side of station. One was blinded the other had his foot blown clean off.

Had them escorted to ambulance which was waiting by mule bridge. Neville came round during afternoon. Laurence Rook goes over to Campo to relieve John Shaw. He had a big welcome there, and the proceedings somewhat harrassed his recce, so he said! Think that we shall be going to Campo tomorrow, but should hear early.

2330 hrs. Laurence reports Germans in Popoli, but clear of Sulmona. Many German P.O.W.s about whom he is rounding up. Also 4 British P.O.W.s there should be back in Palena tomorrow.

There has been a general move on the Adriatic side, to our right and contact has been lost so we are informed. It is thought that the enemy have fallen right back to the line of the Pescara river.

Meantime, Douro learns his friend Astor, wounded in the shoulder, is a prisoner, while his driver, Cpl Manseargh, has been killed. But it is impossible to give pursuit. HCR headquarters moves to Casoli where Colonel Gooch is given overall command of D Force, comprising his own regiment, the 9th Manchesters, Central India Horse and 85 Mountain Regiment RA. 700 men of 1HCR have been spread over a front of more than 10 miles.

It takes 6 gallons of petrol every evening to charge the batteries of the rear and side links – that is to say, the wireless sets which communicate with D Force Headquarters and with the troops on either flank. There is constant communication over this rear link every day in order to ensure that everybody gets fed and supplied with ammunition and so forth. For the next five more days they are still on foot. Next stop Sulmona.

***

Astor describes the utterly unforeseen sequel to his search for Gooch near Gamberale:

> We have hardly moved forward when a volley of shots came from the wood on our left. 'What was that?' I asked as Rossiter stopped the jeep. 'That must be the Jerries Sir,' as some more shots rang out. I could see it was by then. Germans in their field grey uniforms appeared on all sides about 30 yards away. I seized my automatic pistol and fired a couple of rounds out of the back window, but the Bosch were closing right in around us and alternatively firing short bursts of MG and MP at us and shouting 'Stop shooting! Get out!'

The Germans are heavily armed:

> Rossiter was hit in the thigh – I couldn't see how badly – and, as we discovered later had a bullet through his left breast pocket. I had an MP bullet in my right arm and two others graze my forehead and right breast. Amid shouts of 'Komm! Get out! For you the war is ended,' I scrambled out of the jeep. Corporal Manseargh, who has been riding about 50 yards behind was untouched, but his motorbike was badly shot up.
>
> As the Bosch ransacked our kit, put a Tellermine under the jeep, and applied field dressings, it felt as if the bottom has fallen out of our little world!

Astor is taken first to Palena Station and now it is his turn to be interrogated. He is fed, given cigarettes, and Italian wine. His captors brag the score is even from the day before when they had a sergeant and two men captured by the Regiment. They learn at once from the log he carries that he is the Intelligence Officer but fortunately he is without his diary. Straightaway he is measuring up his chances to escape, but he has three armed guards constantly watching him. Astor speaks German fluently and he has the respect of his captors at once, who even lend him 'a luscious, fur-lined coat' for the drive by open car to Sulmona gaol. His guards are 'young and gigglish'. One is 18 and has already been in the army a year, and Astor feels they have little love for their officers, but they might easily press the trigger if he makes a run for it.

Sulmona is deserted except for German piquets on street corners. The scene is desolate – every bridge and culvert is ready to be blown up, while horse-drawn vehicles and mules carrying rations are 'driven by elderly Bismarckian figures'. Astor banters in German with his interrogators who ask 'Why are the English at war with Germany?' and other friendly queries calculated to soften him up. One is an apparently loathsome, rat-like German, dressed in camouflage suit and cap; another a grubby-looking Italian civilian aged about 30, who is friendly and asks personal questions in French.

When the German leaves Astor asks the Italian how they stood, and in a jocular way, 'How the hell one could escape from here?' The Italian, a Corsican, says he will help if he can in any way – to escape or provide food – but that the Germans distrust them, and supervise them closely.

Astor is stripped of his possessions and locked in a cell. An hour or so later it is morning and Astor is miserable, as it is his 26th birthday. He is woken by a heavy tramp of feet and taken down once again to be questioned, this time in English by an 'insignificant little German'.

For half an hour he tried to impress me by what he already knew – or thought he knew, and pumped me for information and confirmation. 'What were you doing at Gamberale?' 'What were the armoured cars doing which we saw moving along the ridge two days ago?' 'Why were the Allies not attacking in this sector?' 'How much armour had we got in this sector?' 'What use could it serve in the mountains?' 'What were "Big ones"? "Little ones" and "Ants"?'

Eventually he realised that he had got all the information he was going to get – namely, rank and number and so dismissed me by saying, 'You know we have ways of making our prisoners talk. Are you sure you will not change your mind and answer my questions?'

Pressure on Astor continues, with pleasant breaks for several days when he meets other prisoners or is fed cherries and cigarettes by the Italians. He is so relieved Gooch was not captured, as he so easily might have been, and he wonders what his comrades will think when they find his blown-up jeep – a mine or an ambush? The interrogators continue for two more days trying to wear down his resistance:

I was confronted by the ratty looking German, still in his camouflage suit, and another arrogant young officer of the bullying type, chewing a cheap cigar as he lent back in his chair with his feet on the desk. The rat spoke first. 'This officer must know the answers to a few questions. He's got no time to waste, so, kindly answer them immediately.' I gave my name, rank and number and suggested that there was no need for the officer to waste any more time as that was all the information he was going to get. He flew into a furious tirade, shouted, barked and puffed at his cigar. 'As far as I'm concerned, you're a spy,' he said. 'Nobody but a spy could be in the area of Gamberale dressed like that.' 'How do you deal with spies in the British army?' he asked. I said that I was not a spy, but an officer in the British army, as he could see by my uniform.

They put some more questions to me but obtaining no answer shouted 'Come along now, you are wasting our time! We will give you five minutes to think it over. That is your last chance. If you do not change your mind then you may regret it.'

I was marched out into a small courtyard. The sun was shining brightly and reflecting light and heat off the marble floor. Even so I could feel my teeth chattering, and the hairs on my body standing up through gooseflesh, due as much to my rage as any feeling of fear ... Me a spy; do I know what the penalty for spies is? Yes, of course: death. What if they shoot me? It can't be such a bad way of dying. In any case, it's my duty as a British officer to tell these bastards nothing, no matter what extremes they go to at intimidation.

Presently I was called back in. 'Well, what have you decided?' I gave them my name, rank and number once again. 'Bah we know that! So you won't talk! At that moment there was a rifle shot just outside. 'Did you hear that?' 'Yes.' 'Well, that's how we deal with spies. Are you going to answer these questions?' 'No.' 'Very well, then. It is your own choice. I'm afraid you will regret it.'

I was then marched back to my cell where I washed and lay on the bed. During the course of the afternoon I was given a receipt for my confiscated money and the Italian prison guards looked in from time to time and seemed friendly, but of course one never can be sure with Italians. However, they eventually took me down to the first aid room where my slight wounds were dressed by the local Italian civilian doctor.

He then hears, with joy, that Rome has fallen.

***

Ian Van Ammel is on a parallel track to Astor.

We were told only to give rank name and number if caught. So I was moved to a little compound on my own. Lots of barbed wire. Then I was joined by an Indian NCO, a miserable sod. I had nothing to smoke, I was starving, so he wasn't any great cheer. What happened to my Corporal? Halls was kept somewhere, not as an officer.

Suddenly they called me in one evening, marched me in and here was a table full of marvellous food. They said, 'We know who you are.' Our intelligence office Gavin Astor had been ambushed and they had got Gavin. He didn't join us until Austria at a huge transit camp for prisoners of all nationalities.

They gave us a marvellous dinner and sent us on the road to Cassino. We marched up the spine of Italy with the Germans retreating. Hot on the heels was the Battleaxe Division. After the war my brother worked it out with me, they were 45 mins behind us. Germans were marching in 1000s in an orderly retreat. We marched to Lake Tresamino and then they put us in trucks. We marched through Florence at night, we couldn't see it, more's the pity.

There was a town called Terni, at a rail and road junction, where the air raid siren went. They herded us onto a factory building with a roof on it while they all cowed down below in trenches. Along came about 20 Hudson bombers, 500 pound bombs landed right in the centre of Terni, and then they dropped 20 smaller ones and the town of Terni was completely obliterated. They killed civilians, they buggered the network of roads and railways. Then we went into trucks to Mantua – they gave me my first possession – you own nothing as a POW – not even a cigarette.

126

An Italian orderly gave me a toothbrush. I got the most awful foot rot, 'twigged toes', on this march. He gave me a thing called sulphamohyde powder which cured it in no time – amazing – I have always been grateful to that little Italian. One night someone crept in, a German, and he stole my boots – they were too comfortable. They stole my mountain boots, and gave me some Italian boots made of cardboard and two sizes too big.

Astor and Manseargh, like Van Ammel and Halls, share the fate of the retreating Germans. Driven off north-west, they are lodged in insanitary gaols, and by turns starved or well fed. The questioning continues, but as the flight goes on it decreases in intensity and for Astor almost approaches friendly conversation. All the time Italians supply company and laughter, but the food generally is dire: lunch, half a dixie or iron pot of hot greasy water with thick leathery and utterly tasteless macaroni floating about in it. One night Gavin has a drunken German solder locked into his cell and has to share his straw and blankets.

Travelling farther north at night in a civilian car with a captured paratrooper just as dawn is breaking, they have a puncture and jack up their car:

We had not stopped five minutes when the morning flight of six Spitfires appeared over the hills. What could be better! We dived into a culvert leaving the car jacked up in the middle of the road, and there we awaited the inevitable onslaught. It was a pleasure to see how windy the Bosch were. We could not feel the same fear and seemed to disregard the danger, for to us they were still 'Camarades', both having a common enemy. As we squatted under the culvert watching the fighters search out the ground, the whole country seemed to be hypnotized as a field-mouse is by a hovering hawk. Then one of them would catch sight of a vehicle which had been badly camouflaged or inadequately concealed. The leader would peel off, then the second, third, fourth aircraft into a vertical dive. We could hear the cannon guns and see the clouds of smoke coil into the air as four vehicles were similarly dealt with. Then came our turn ... From left and right and back and front they swooped and dived as they pumped AP shells into our stranded vehicle. After it has been satisfactorily dealt with, the next vehicle, barely a mile further along the road, received the same treatment. It happened to be a petrol lorry, and burnt beautifully! By now our silence has been broken and cigarettes were circulating. We scrambled out of the hole and examined the vehicle. Sure enough it was 'Kaput'. Every tyre was punctured, the glass broken and radiator, engine, and body riddled with shell holes.

The providential puncture had spared them the strafing. They proceeded on foot. Gavin notices how the Germans post 'air [raid] sentries' on the running boards of their transport, and cover it with whole trees and branches when they can. In daylight they stick red cross markings on store and ammunition lorries; he and fellow captives pass burntout vehicles at intervals 'still smouldering while their crews sat by and laughed and shouted "Kaput!"'

It is an apocalyptic scene: towns are dive bombed and evacuated, crossroads decorated with a hundred different and confusing signs. Astor shelters on equal terms with German officers, crouching behind walls, 'quite friendly and full of respect as indeed they all were when they saw we were English'. He wonders how they can go on fighting. Why were they doing this? When losing the war, taking prisoners with them, while obeying their inevitable orders to withdraw?

> They all looked a wretched, hunted, underfed, ill-clad lot of men; hardly a happy face on any of them and no two dressed alike. Their transport was in a shocking condition and appeared to do without any maintenance. All the lorries were overloaded; many of the cars had no tyres and were running on bare rims; while a tremendous portion of course were on tow.

Still the rules of war are followed. But when 170 Italian prisoners escape from a jail in Perugia the prison commander orders the remaining 700 to be led out into the woods and liquidated; fortunately this never happens. The Allied prisoners are paraded with their hands up, but when Astor as the senior officer explains they are not Italians, the drunken guards apologise and thrust cigarettes at them, saying what a pity it is the English and Germans are fighting one another, they should be fighting the Russians. At one point on the northward trek, with the Germans still determined not to leave them behind – they are war booty, tokens of German superiority – they, Astor and nine others, even have to find their own transport. He endeavours to convince his companions it is worth making a dash for it and escaping to the mountains:

Unfortunately they were all against it. One man had already spent five months wandering about the mountains; another had been living with Italians in the hills since the armistice. They both felt it was not worth it. Another was frightened about what reprisals might be taken, while all the Yanks thought about was getting to the PW cage and the red X food parcels. I knew nothing about red X food parcels and their contents so could not appreciate their attraction! But they were all unanimously opposed to escaping which was most regrettable, as I felt that there was a good chance, probably our last chance, of making a successful attempt.

And so they join the rout once again:

> After dark, a lorry arrived and together with all the household furniture and most of the staff we were bundled on board and set off for the next 'stately home' which the firm had taken over for itself still farther back. As soon as the light failed every wood and field sprang to life revealing troops, horses, guns, limbers, tanks and vehicles, which immediately crowded onto the road and renewed their northerly procession. There was no attempt at traffic control. Everything was packed tightly, nose to croup. Progress was reduced to barely 1 mile an hour. There seemed to be no unit or formations as such, but a tank here, a 10-ton lorry there, half a dozen horse-drawn limber somewhere else, with motorcycles, staff cars and self-propelled guns thrown in willy-nilly. How anybody knew who belonged to what or who was bound to where, I can't imagine! But on they went slowly and determinedly like a stream of ants, shouting and yelling at the top of their voices.

Astor progresses in lorry and then motor coach through Florence and Bologna with sick prisoners suffering from malaria, dysentery, diarrhoea, and one with pneumonia. The bouncy, bullying NCO in charge refuses to stop the coach and let them urinate, only doing so finally in town centres when civilians, women and so on are walking about. 'This seemed very typical of the German mentality, to feel superior and to satisfy their sadistic instincts; the more so as they knew what these men were suffering from.' Finally reaching the 'haven' of the well fortified and stable northern Italy, Astor is entrained in a cattle truck en route for Germany. The truck is divided; twenty prisoners on one side and nine guards on the other. They 'displayed the common German trait of gaining a false feeling of superiority by eating their rations in front of us in a gloating manner, as we had only a small hunk of bread each. At first they refuse to talk to us, but as time went on and the monotony of the journey wore upon us, I succeeded in getting them to talk, and finally they handed food and cigarettes through the wire.'

They still believe, or so they say, that Germany will win the war and that London is burning, while the second front is not mentioned at all. So begins Astor's period of 'in the bag'.

CHAPTER TWELVE

FEMINA MORTA

One hour of life crowded to the full with glorious action, and filled with noble risks, is worth whole years of those mean observances of paltry tedium, in which men step through existence, like sluggish waters through a marsh, without either honour or observation.

Sir Walter Scott

The suffering of anti-fascist Italians, especially those who had suffered in Rome before its liberation by Mark Clark's American troops, should never be forgotten. They had already had 22 years of Fascism, during which, as expressed by the film director Luchino Visconti, Italians had been suffocated, crushed by dictatorship, to the point where nothing true or genuine existed any more. But then, when Italy changed sides in September 1943, 'Rome suffered nine months which were a paroxysm of horror.'

General Kesselring had narrowly missed death at his headquarters in Frascati when 130 US B-17s bombed and obliterated the vineyard town killing 2,000 civilians and dozens of German staff. He threatened to raze Rome to the ground, but did not carry this out. By late January, when the Anzio landings added to the complications rather than solution of the march on Rome, Kesselring was north-east of Rome in a command post in the Sabine Hills. The flooding of the Pontine marshes with seawater and the subsequent breeding of mosquito larvae in this brackish water slowed down the advance out of Anzio, but then the capture of Rome depended on Cassino falling in May 1944.

In Rome itself communist guerrillas blew up an SS barracks on Via Rasella and killed thirty-two Germans. In the reprisals on Kesselring's order that followed, ten captured communists for every German, altogether 335 prisoners, were executed in the Ardeantine Pits, a quarry near the Catacombs. The Germans blasted out the rock face to conceal the bodies, but there was one witness who later testified at the trial of Kesselring at Nuremburg.

On June 4, while the Republican Guards hurriedly shed their Fascist insignia, replacing them with little stars of the free Italy, the Germans in retreat, black and bloody, bundled Italian prisoners into their trucks or took pot shots at them. Panzer tanks fled over the Sisto Bridge, the only one still open, while beneath it boys swam and sunbathed. One Roman recalled a little Wehrmacht soldier aged about fifteen holding in one hand a cluster of bombs, in the other three or four ice-cream cones. That evening Romans thronged the Via Veneto area and celebrated 'with wild unbridled joy, radiant with solidarity'. American loudspeaker trucks announced the landings in Normandy.

The Germans were now on the move north, and the Regiment senses their movement out of forward positions they hold: now is the time to probe further and to pursue. The stalemate is over: adventure, excitement are in the air, the exhilarating hue and cry after a retreating enemy. Fraser:

> *Tuesday June 6.* Heard at 9.30 this morning that the second front has begun. Great news. Eighth Army Tps are also 10 miles north of Rome whose capture was announced yesterday morning ...
>
> ... About 30 shells fell in front of Sqn HQ about 8.15pm for no apparent reason. Also a guerrilla patrol had a battle with 5 Germans at the bottom of the Lettopalena Gorge. As far as we could gather they got at least one and possibly two.
>
> 'Stand-to' 8.45 – 09.45pm. Slept a lot during afternoon. News coming through about 2nd front still good. 11,000 front line planes used. 4,000 ships and thousands of other crafts, really amazing – I wonder what day 2HCR will go across. Bridgehead evidently well established between Le Havre and Cherbourg. Caen captured. No patrols out tonight.

Next day is quiet and recuperative for Fraser: washing, sweeping out his billet, reading and sleeping – and a 'very successful war against the flies with flit and swatters!! There are thousands of them everywhere.' It is another lovely day until 10pm when a patrol is cancelled. But then:

> Just heard that a B sqn Patrol under Domski Revertera was chased down the mountains above Fara. They had a running fight to within 200 yds of the road. Domski was very badly wounded, and had to be left on the hill in a dying condition. Two others were wounded, otherwise all got back ok. This brings the total of officers killed and missing to four.

The episode on June 7, when Lieutenant Dominic Revertera of B Squadron with his Corporal Sherwin and five troopers pursued the Germans on Revertera's initiative, is a paradigm of the whole mad tragedy of this European war.

Domski, as his fellow officers called him, was born in Vienna, the cradle of Hitler's Nazism. His father was Graf Von Revertera, whose brother, a leading Austrian politician, was a victim of the Nazi *Anschluss* of 1938 when Hitler annexed Austria. Not surprisingly Domski, who fled to London, became an implacable anti-Nazi.

Given the pre-war link between the continental European aristocracy and the English, Domski was well known to the Carnarvon family for one especially interesting reason, which is frequently referred to in Porchey's letters home to his father. Porchey first mentions Domski in connection with Tilly Losch, his father's second wife, from whom Carnarvon is seeking a divorce. Tilly, an attractive and gifted actress and dancer, who later became a painter, was married before Carnarvon to Edward James, the Anglo-American millionaire and surrealist art patron, who founded a ballet company for her. She danced with Balanchine and became the mistress of Tom Mitford, brother of the Mitford sisters. While James was her husband at Monkton he had her wet footprints as she emerged from the bath woven into the carpet of the spiral stairs. These can still be seen at West Dean, to which James moved the carpet.

Five years after James divorced her for adultery with Prince Serge Obolensky, Tilly fell into a severe clinical depression, gave up dancing and attended a sanatorium in Switzerland. It was here that she met Henry Carnarvon, who in 1939 married her, and mindful of her health sent her to America to avoid the war, where she began further affairs. Here she started to paint, first exhibiting in New York in 1944. That this domestic thread of marital intrigue and infidelity should be illuminated by Domski's presence in the Regiment sheds an intriguing sidelight on the Highclere family. Later her works were bought by the Tate and other galleries.

On February 19 Porchey writes, 'Valerian knows Tilly quite well and spent early 1939 in Switzerland with her in a hospital. He is nice and just got married out here about three weeks ago. Also Domski Revertera, who is an Austrian and knew her both in England and in Austria and is very interesting about her.' At this point Porchey's mind veers off into snipe and duck shooting, and the matter is dropped.

However, only weeks later, Porchey, who has just been duck shooting once more with Valerian, brings up the subject again, this time more fully:

> As regards to Domski Revertera's knowledge of Tilly's past and present he is sick and has not been able to delve fully, but he said – she was a low class Jewish girl who through a nobleman got a chance on the stage as a danc-ing girl aged 18 – she was kept and lived with the nobleman and soon rose to heights with her dancing. She is typical of many others and soon left this man and made her way to Europe where apparently he [Domski] met her and saw her often on the stage. He thinks her very pretty and a marvellous dancer but a b--! in some ways.

Porchey feels his separated parents' pain at his being away (and his sister Jeanne is absent too): 'Poor darling Pups you must be very lonely and Mum also.'

The reason is, as becomes clear, because Lord Carnarvon has decided to divorce her – this is never spelt out but may easily be guessed – and Porchey clearly wants to detach his father from this fortune hunter. On March 20 he communicates, 'Can get more news from Domsky Revertera about Tilly.'

On April 28 Porchey writes to Mrs Geoffrey Grenfell, his divorced mother who has remarried: in the midst of all the racing and betting news (and communicating with her about his father) – 'Papa got me 500-15 for 2000G's present price 16-1 will be 10-1 if Harry Wragg rides him so you will see it is a good price – 133-1... I understand Tilly is now very "LATE" and in her near future the "late" Lady C. (It seems Pups has been seeing Lady D. who "keeps him company"). About this silence is essential.'

It does not remain so for long. Now in Italy, Porchey expresses his regret at being in the Italian heights and not being back in Cairo eating good food at the Union Bar, the Union Club and the Cecil and Petit Coin de France (it seems his separated mother and father may even sometimes compete over who sends him more letters). But first it is Carnarvon who gives Porchey some other news on June 6, D-Day. First he says he has heard that Porchey's CO, Wispy, has written flattering letters to Colonel Andrew Ferguson about Porchey – 'You have been marked out as an outstanding officer'. He then goes on to bring Porchey up-to-date on his divorce proceedings:

> [Colonel] Rogers said that he had not seen Tilly, but understood her exhi-
> bition had been quite successful, as far as that sort of thing can be termed
> successful, that she was leading a very good and quiet life amongst a
> few friends of her own Bohemian circle, otherwise, he had no news to
> tell about her. I went to the M. of I. [Ministry of Information] this morn-
> ing, and they kindly consented to forward the writ to be served on her by
> the speediest air transport, and I hope to hear from the Solicitors in New
> York within the week that they have accomplished their mission. Tilly, as
> you know, is given 60 days after the receipt of the writ in which she can
> elect to defend the case, and so there will be quite a time lag, before we
> know whether she is going to fight or whether she will let the matter go
> by default. All this is very troublesome, and is not conducive to improving
> my peace of mind.
>   Jeanne sends you lots of love.
>   The racing at Windsor on Saturday was not very exciting.

As soon as he receives this, Porchey writes to his mother, confessing violent hatred towards the woman who, we assume, has caused the break-up of his parents' marriage and led his father a dance. 'I hope Tilly's case is finished as soon as possible. I fear she will contest but I fancy will be too frightened by public opinion to return if she did. I would like to turn a Tommy Gun on her and would not miss!' It is this same letter in which Porchey reports the death of Domski – 'I cannot say how.'

Domski is also a close friend of Herbert: again with pre-war connections. According to Herbert, Domski was of medium height, had crinkly hair and blue-grey eyes and was very good-looking.

> Domski was an Austrian and we have photos of him dressed in *lederho-*
> *sen*. My sister Renée was in a car going to Austria to listen to music in

135

summer 1938. Domski had to keep a low profile because he fell in love with my sister and proposed marriage, and although she liked him as a friend she didn't want to marry him – it was not what she was after, and he was already engaged so she wasn't interested. He came as a refugee to England with a Russian prince called Pashkov, who was extremely good looking with a very good operatic voice, so my second sister fell in love with Pashkov – so we had a left and right there. She would have said yes if he had wanted marriage. Domski took a job making or distributing torch batteries, something to keep body and soul together. He was a frequent visitor to our flat in London and we lost touch for I was doing a law degree and then joined the Regiment. When I got to Italy I was amazed to hear Domski had arrived in B Squadron. I hardly had time to talk to him because we were in separate squadrons, which were never grouped together in a regimental mess until the end of the war.

Throughout May, Domski is leading patrols into the heights. In those first five or six days of June the exchanges of fire draw more casualties.

1   Patrol under Lieut H.R. du Plessis returned reporting that rd Montenerodomo to br over Sangro river at H/270698 badly blown along whole route. No further infm ref Lieut. Astor. Patrol under Lieut. Williams to area H/1188 returned. Enemy move seen on Tavella Rotunda C Sqn recced area Pizzoferrato with a view to moving in during night.
2   C Sqn completed move into Pizzoferrato by 0230 hrs leaving ech at H/280620. Patrol under Lieut. Lord Porchester to recce area around burnt out Jeep of Lieut. Astor's at H/158682. NTR. Patrol under Lieut. A.L. Rook returned 2055hrs with a German WO PW captured in his OP at H/105678. The PW was from 661 Arty Regt and with him were taken marked maps, gun posns and ref codes. During the night 2/3 Tp 58 Med RA came up to engage enemy guns located, the following day.
3   Taken with the German PW on 2 Jun was a marked map, locations of his bty posns and DF tasks these arrived at a very opportune moment as they were carefully studied by RA Offrs before the Tp 58 Med had their shoot. At 1500 hrs Tp Med Regt started shooting at targets in areas Colle di Cocci Campo Di Giove, Pescocostanzo, and Palena Stn. In all 320 shells were fired and according to air OP were very accurate. There was no CB fire from the enemy. Lieut. Crosfield's patrol returned and reported enemy post of two secs in area H/094810, OO Nos 6,7 issued.

4   During the whole day there were continuous explosions in the enemy line indicating possible demolitions before withdrawal. Patrols reported NMS on whole front. Sqns ordered to send patrols fwd to ascertain whether the enemy were withdrawing or not.

5   Explosions continued all along front during the night. A patrol from B Sqn under Lieut. E. G. Wood Hill reported enemy still on Majella mtn but much fewer in number. An A Sqn patrol to Colle di Cocci reported NMS. A C Sqn patrol under Lieut. J.F.A. Roberts reported Palena St clear of enemy. Lieut. Roberts and Cpl Price were unfortunately killed by a mine while returning from Palena Stn. Tpr Rogers was wounded also by the same explosion.

6   From the report found on Lieut. Roberts it appears the enemy have started to withdraw. A fwd patrol base of 1 Offr and 20 ORs formed at H/103677 to patrol fwd. During the night, a patrol under Lieut. Lamb, IO D Force, Lieut. Brayne-Nicholls, 4 ORs and 25 Partisans to Colle di Cocci area to discover if enemy still in posn. The patrol proceeded up the North side of Colle in order to be able to look down into it. They found that some of the fwd MG posts were unocc, but that the enemy were still in posn behind the hill. At 1330 hrs the enemy shelled Palena area, no cas. A further patrol under Lieut. S.B. Woollard sent up to H/097858 to observe enemy posn in that area.

7   2030 Approx 30 shells on Palena area.

Domski's state of mind exceeds the Regimental brief and ethos. His blood is up, and he becomes, or is propelled into what Karl Marlantes calls 'a transcendent state'. First, Domski and his five-man patrol move down a valley running south alongside Monte Amaro with the fateful name of *Femina Morta*: seeing no enemy they climb Monte Amaro to reconnoitre the German position overlooking Lama.

On the Maiella Lieut. Woollard's and Lieut. Revertera's patrols reported that enemy had withdrawn from their fwd posns but were still holding Pt 2793 at H/071869, where there is a holding at Pt 2793 at H/071869, where there are two stone houses or huts in which there is a radio locn stn. Lieut. Revertera's patrol was attacked by an enemy patrol of 12 men, Lieut. Revertera was mortally wounded in the stomach and the patrol, after dragging him for 600yds were forced to leave him. The enemy chased the patrol down the mtn to withn a mile of the Lama-Palena rd. In the South C Sqn sent two OPs reported their areas clear of enemy. During the day continuous explosions along the whole front, giving every indication that the enemy is preparing to withdraw.

Domski's bravery, his vast and foolhardy desire to pursue, to get even, resulted in his death. Had he waited, he would be alive and a possible contributor to this account. Clearly, however, he was possessed with rage and broke the Regiment's rules.

The platoon officer Karl Marlantes reports a similar experience in the Vietnam War. Survival also means guilt, although this was rare in British forces in the Second World War:

> I shall probably never be as thrilled as I was that one moment I left a safe position to join my old platoon in the assault when I ended up trying to pull Utter from underneath the machine gun. I ran toward the fighting with the same excitement, trembling and thrill as a lover rushing to the beloved in the spiritual love poetry of the mystics. Perhaps these are identical transcendent psychological states. But I don't ever want to do it again. It is a dangerous inflated state of being.

Marlantes was fortunate: he survived, Domski didn't. 'His fanatical hatred of the Nazis and all their works,' says Colonel The Hon. Humphrey Wyndham, MC, in his history of the Regiment, 'made it impossible for him ever to resist the temptation to try to get at them ... he allowed his brave and warlike spirit to lead him into doing something which he was not supposed to do: he pushed on above the snow line and encountered an enemy ski patrol. In the engagement that followed he was hit in the stomach and very shortly afterwards died.'

The greater irony, pointing to the eternal tragedy of war, is yet to come. First, respect and camaraderie shows itself in the energy shown by his fellow officers to find and retrieve Domski's body and make sure it is properly buried. Two days later a patrol led by Lt. Tree is dispatched to try and find his body, but Monte Amaro is covered all day by a mist and this proves impossible.

By this time A and B Squadrons, now trained by German-speaking ski and mountain warfare instructors, should be following up the Germans' retreat, but with characteristic thoroughness and because, too, of the mountainous terrain, all roads and tracks have been blown up and heavily mined. The Regiment has already suffered serious casualties from minefields. They proceed slowly.

Only on June 11 does another patrol find Domski's body. Douro tells the author how his Corporal

> ... carried him on his back quite a long way ... He was apparently dead, reluctantly he put him down. If he hadn't his whole troop would have been killed [Corporal Sherwin fought a rearguard action and was awarded an immediate Military Medal.] When we advanced I didn't actually see it, but they found he had been buried by the German mountain division with a cross made of broken skis, and on the cross was written – I think in English – 'In memory of a brave Austrian'.

The ski troops were Austrian – the same who had taken Van Ammel – and realised he was a fellow national, they could even have discovered he was from a well-known family. Brother was killing brother.

Domski's death is passed over quickly: it somehow goes deep – yet no one at the time wants to linger too long over this tragedy. Fraser simply reports 'Domski killed (shot).' Shaw writes: 'This afternoon heard that Domski had been killed on the mountain.'

Ewart is involved with learning how to load and fire a 75mm gun as he now has taken charge with little training of one of Heavy Troop's two guns: 'Heard that Domski Revertera had been killed, must be getting hardened as this shocked me for a very little time. One seems to take it for granted ... Got back to our neat house at Fallascoso. Gun is now all right and spent afternoon working out how we can improvise to fire indirectly.'

> *Saturday June 10.* Went to bed 3 in morning and got Cpl Major Turner to begin to make a plumb line for measuring elevation on guns. Then back here where Cpl Winter is going to make the traverse strings. Half holiday in afternoon. Teddy and Dent went off to Palena. Rang up Dickie Crosfield this evening and he says clinometers have arrived but dials will be some time. Hope to fire guns by Monday and to begin to get some sort of efficiency by then. Porchey went up hill to look for trace of Ian or Cpl Halls but found nothing.

CHAPTER THIRTEEN

GAMES WITH A GOOSE

A major reason why warfare is an intractable human problem and so difficult to put a stop to. It offers us raw life: vibrant, terrifying and full blast. We are lifted into something larger than ourselves. If it were all bad, there would be much less of it, but war simply isn't all bad. Why do kids play war games? Why do adults enter professions such as ambulance drivers, search and rescue, firefighters? Because these activities lift you from your limited world.

Karl Marlantes, *What it is like to go to war*

The Regiment now joins its armoured vehicles again after the six weeks in Monte Amaro's shadow and is ready to move forward. Before they mount on wheels they still have several footslogging episodes to endure. There are unexpected dangers and the random workings of chance in an enemy's retreat. Forcing a retreat is not exactly victory, and the Second World War exemplifies in terms of the world's future history Napoleon's dictum that often the most dangerous moments come with victory.

Colonel Gooch is now Commander of all D Force, but to his young and even then it seems slightly eccentric Signals Officer, Lieutenant the Lord Uxbridge, he is remembered as a security risk:

I was Signals Officer in the Armoured Car and I had better tell you before I forget. We all thought he was very old – about 50! Typical! He was very bad on security so when people said B Squadron should move to the right

I snatched away the Colonel's microphone and he laughed – we all did – but the fact that the Signals Officer was tearing away the mike the Colonel was talking on is surprising – but I had to!

Wispy has further quirks that amuse Henry: not only 'oldish by the standards of the day' but also 'he brought his own bath with him, and his manservant [Hope] gave him a good bath when they were sufficiently quiet! Two or three occasions when we were moving forward he managed to get the aerial in the armoured car up his trousers. There was a lot of laughter in the middle of the war, as you can imagine, this happened two or three times before we could get him to understand what to do.'

In the untidy flux of German withdrawal the Regiment tries to pursue, but without assistance from the Royal Engineers to repair the roads it is impossible to 'follow up the enemy and maintain contact with him'. 'Contact' often means casualties, and with Revertera's death and Astor's capture they are apprehensive. On June 10 the Regiment is ordered to send a squadron forward to Sulmona, 17 miles from Palena, which is 'not feasible', yet even so the order is obeyed by Fraser and Rook on patrol with their troops. On June 10 another patrol under Lt Coats reports that Monte Amaro has been evacuated.

Palena is now safe. The bells from the church had been stolen by the Germans to melt down for armaments, but the St Falco relics have survived, for the precious saint's skull and other relics were hidden in that silver statue and this had been secretly built into the bell tower walls and therefore concealed. Today, Palena still celebrates her saint every year when her people carry the sacred relic in procession through the town.

All the diaries register excitement at this time. But both Shaw and Lt. Rook have been missing Herbert: he here takes up the thread about his disappearance.

You said about Gavin Astor being put in the bag. I have a bit of a story about that. A Squadron was in reserve ... While we were in reserve Tony sent me out on a mission to mark on a map all the points between us and the village where Gavin was taken prisoner. He mis-estimated the time (two hours), it took me all day. It was nightfall when I got there and I did not find the relief crew of the people who were leaving. It was a sister regiment of some sort. Gavin was on his way there when he was put in

141

the bag by the Germans. I got to his place at night and the local Italians said Tedeschi had just left. But they could come back so we set a guard for the night and all promptly fell asleep as we were exhausted and slept till early morning. We were then relieved by members of C Squadron. When ultimately I got back I found all my kit had been distributed among my fellow officers! Frankie Williams once found all his kit missing because he'd been put in the bag but it was only temporary and he managed to escape. The vultures had been! I'd only just received 200 Three Castle cigarettes, very posh! And they were the first to go!

The Italian crowds, delirious with joy over liberation, present their own problems, as Shaw notes on June 8: 'I duly left with 18 of my troop and thirty-odd partisans. After a long climb we eventually arrived at Cocci at about five in the morning, very cold. It was anyhow clear of Germans but there were a few scattered mines.' The next day they go down into Campo di Giove, where they have a terrific reception. 'All the village turned out with flowers and vino and eggs – all very disconcerting and embarrassing. Laid flowers on the last war memorial and tried to take up precautionary positions but locals crowded round and made it very difficult.'

After breakfast Shaw goes on to Causano with Tpr Haley and two partisans, and they are met on the way by masses of 'boys etc. from Causano' and had another even more elaborate floral reception, and more memorials, and had to give a speech from the balcony of the Municipio. 'Was sat down in the main street to drink and was given too much. Rode a horse back to Campo and eventually after a fearful walk got back to Palena. Collected one German in Campo.' By now Shaw's troop is feeling the strain:

Troop very tired but ok myself. Tony and Malcolm going to Campo today. Laurence went yesterday. I get the job of recceing another better track to Campo, up right of Cocci, and lifting mines on it. Set out at two with C of H Collet, Cpl Hawkin and three others. Much better track, lifted an 'S' [*Schu*] mine to clear track just rear of the crest and arrived at Campo by quarter to five. Tony arrived soon after. Tea with the nuns in Campo. Took over a very nice house and had a good night's rest. Cpl Westcott returned from Pacentro, where he was welcomed by the town band, with one Jugoslav. Collet then returned from Caramanico, where he was given a sort of civic lunch, with Brit ex POW and 2 Russian ex POW. No news of Lawrence other than Sulmona.

Shaw is furious when he hears of Rook's capture:

Man from Sulmona arrived early saying Laurence and Yorkman [the interpreter he calls 'odd'] in the bag. Tony set out to Sulmona at eight to see the place and confirm about Laurence, Malcolm and tp followed him. I returned to Palena with a motley assortment of ex POW's, Russians, J-S's, Poles and Ities. Got back in 2½ hours myself, others came in gradually. No more news of Laurence, but reported fighting at Poludi and 50 partisans from Sulmona gone as reinforcements. Neville set off for Campo, also Herbert. Teddy in Palena. Lamb furious with Yorkman and up here with an assistant. Apparently taking over Sulmona sector, we are probably being withdrawn. What a bloody nuisance.

Fraser and his troop meet Shaw in Campo di Giove on Saturday 10 June. Fraser:

Move off up mountain over Sugar Loaf Hill at 2.15pm with Tp and 6 mules. The Hell of a Climb! – 1650 metres, taking about 2½ hrs in all, very steep indeed, both sides. Not very fit owing to the fact of having been shut up in Palena since Monday night. Arrive Campo di Giovi at 7.00pm. Entertained to tea by the nuns with lovely hot chocolate and iced cake. ... Two 3 Tp. patrols return from Pcentro and Caramanico with P.O.W.'s during the night. Both English and Russian!!

Herbert's account consolidates the story and vindicates what Shaw is assigned to do next:

I cannot remember exactly how A Squadron was to get itself from Palena to Sulmona, but the essential details are anchored in my memory: firstly, the way forward for the Squadron was to be reconnoitered by John Shaw and his close support troop (infantry normally mounted in half-track scout cars but now on foot like the rest of us); he would be first to enter Sulmona and would then declare it clear for the Squadron.

I had an independent mission as signals officer, which was to get my heavy transmitting wireless set and its supporting batteries (massively heavy) to Sulmona on mule back, so as to provide communications from Sulmona to the rear of our party. I was allocated two pack mules and their Indian muleteers. The first mule carried the wireless set on one side balanced by a battery on the other side; the second mule was made to carry two batteries, one on either side. Pack mules had to carry with them a minimum amount of fodder for such an expedition and this also was stowed and balanced with the rest.

Besides the muleteers my little party included three men, not forgetting the ubiquitous trooper Freeman, my soldier servant. I would be independent of John Shaw's troop because mules couldn't go where men went. Thus it was that one morning at sunrise I left Palena and the rest of A Squadron behind me and started to pick my way forward, happy and excited to be on my own with a mission to fulfil. The feature which faced me and had to be crossed was a spur running down from Monte Amaro 2800 metres up on my right front, to Monte Porrara 2100 metres high on my left; and as Palena was itself on the 1000 metres contour line the actual height I had to climb, between the two, was perhaps two or three hundred metres.

I went at a fast pace, anxious to get on. As the crow flies Palena was no more than about five miles from my destination at Sulmona, but there were no set paths and I would be picking my way up a mountain side through wooded country. I steered a zigzag course, with my mules in mind. By early afternoon we had picked up a footpath of sorts on the way up and there was a point where it had been cut through the side of the mountain so that the ground rose steeply up on one side, and dropped about eight feet on the other, to a little plateau. The first mule went through the narrow point without a hitch but the second mule, with a load spread a little wider on its sides, just touched the high ground on one side, enough to overbalance, and it rolled down on the plateau ending up on its back pinned down by the weight of its load, all four legs in the air. We rushed to its aid, someone holding its head and trying to calm it down and the rest of us clawing at the girth buckles to free the poor beast of its load, while keeping out of the way of its flailing hooves. Eventually we succeeded and helped it to its feet. There was an uneasy silence while we wondered if it would be in a fit state to continue but we needn't have worried: it shook itself and gave every indication of being perfectly fit.

Once at the crest we took a good rest, relieved that it was still early in the day and that Sulmona lay clearly visible in the distance. It was fairly obvious by now that there could be no Germans about since there we were in broad daylight within reach of our target and still unchallenged. But one danger still lurked: those wretched land mines, which were virtually impossible to detect. At least they blew a leg off, at the worst they killed the unwary painfully and without warning.

We quickly picked up the road which starts halfway down the side of the mountain as a track and becomes more defined as it proceeds. Soon the first street children caught sight of us, their eyes huge when they saw us, and they ran back to spread the news. By the time we reached the first houses of the town itself there was quite a little welcoming crowd, almost all women and children, with fruit, flowers, flasks of wine. And I heard the cry of amazement as we approached: *Indiani! Indiani!* Then we were being hugged and patted on the back, and loaded with presents. '*Tedeschi?* The Germans?' I asked. 'All gone,' they replied happily. 'But where are the others?' they asked.

Talking of the jail, these Italians with red foulards, they were taking some miserable creature off and they were going to shoot him. But I said, surely you should take him to jail, so he could get a fair trial. They thought about this and because I was British they had some respect for me so I got him back and I probably saved his life.

Years later a young nephew of mine asked if I shot any Germans, I said, 'No, I didn't kill any but I did save someone's life.'

The people in Sulmona pressed me. I said that there were lots more of us on the way, arriving any moment. I didn't want it to get back to the wrong people that we were only a handful and very vulnerable. I was taken to the Mayor. I paid my respects and asked for water and stables for my mules.

I set up my transmitter with a long aerial and tried to get through to the Squadron but could get no reply. I wasn't altogether surprised because if they were still on the reverse side of the mountain our equipment was too primitive to work.

We spent the night, the men and I, together in a big room put at our disposal by the mayor, and took it in turns to mount guard, 'just in case'.

The Squadron arrives next day. A Squadron and the town's notables sit down to a civic dinner. Herbert again:

No women at table! They flitted about behind us keeping our plates and glasses full. We were joined at table by a young airman: was he American

145

or British? I cannot remember but I can still see his face, very white from weeks of confinement in an attic while he was kept hidden from the Germans by friendly Italians, who fed him and looked after him at the risk of their lives. What an exciting event it had been to reach Sulmona, and how elating it was to be made so welcome. By then the whole Regiment had fallen in love with Italy.

Shaw's cause for delay is more than a minefield:

> Got up late nothing much to do. About midday Laurence arrived with 6 ex-POWs. Leo came up in the evening to go to Sulmona to see the KDG officer in hospital there. As I wanted to further mark the Cocci minefield, I went over to Campo with him as his guide. Met Lamb and friend on the way and also took an AMGOT floor with us. After dinner at Campo, we all went round to see Nick and the partisans who had invited us to drink vino. Interrupted a tender scene between Nick and the cobbler's daughter. So ended an amusing day.

Fraser is now here in Sulmona too, on June 12, and takes over. They soon find from a list taken from German prisoners in Sulmona indicating that the missing personnel from the Regiment are all POWs.

> Tony and Cpl Major also with us on horses. Walk to Sulmona over the mountains. Arrive 10.15am. Terrific welcome all along the streets when we came in. Almost everyone turned out to clap and cheer us!! Showered with flowers, confetti etc and carried shoulder high for most of the way through the town, proceeded by cars, banners and throngs of civilians. Sulmona was practically undamaged by the Bosch. Eventually arrived at a flat, commandeered for the afternoon, where we shut ourselves in, to reorganize all kit etc.
>
> Found Laurence already in Sulmona having come forward on patrol. Go to Town Hall with him and Tony for drinks and biscuits with the mayor. Excellent marsarilla. Lunch with an 'agent' called 'Marco S' with strawberries, cherries, spaghetti and masses of good food. Best meal for ages. At 3.00 pm move troops down to a house on the north side of the town, prepare to move to Popoli with 6 men and Yorkman.

So for a brief moment some of the officers are again mounted on quadrupeds. Ewart doesn't see much of the forward work, mostly occupied with the diagnostics and technicalities of his 25 pounder for the future advance:

> Left at 8.15 and found the guns near Palena. They seemed very accurate and good guns. Difficulty judging distances up hills as rather complicated. Maths sum has to be worked out. The only way to test the gun is to fire completely indirectly. It remains to be seen how accurate this will be. Did not fire in the place I said I would so got mild rocket from Valerian. In afternoon explained part of it to Cpl Worth and Cpl Lewis. They took rather a long time to understand but eventually they did.

He misses being with the Squadron, and still attends Mass whenever he can. He receives a letter from England that underpins his devotion:

> Getting that letter made me think once more of Beaumont and the fine characters that it produced, so much finer than the majority which are found here. I long to be back there and will probably end up again there anyhow. I am not quite certain about this part but when I look sensibly at the question I know that for me that is the only life. If only one did not have to live in such a completely pagan world. This would be so much easier. One begins to worry over the malevolence of completely unimportant things.

This relieves his constant preoccupation with gunnery detail: brackets, quadrants, locks. But at the spearhead of the advance life is busy and enjoyable:

> Reveille 6.00 am. Go up to see Tony in HQ at 7.00 am. Orders are now to go forward only until 3.00pm this afternoon, to collect information etc. Leave at 9.30am in hired cars for Pratola. I took over a baby Fiat which I drove about! A very good little car!! Arrive in Pratola and having got information, continue on to Rahano – west of Pratola. Another terrific welcome. I was hailed 'English Commandant'. Flowers, clapping and vino in abundance. We were the first English TPs into the town: Collect:
> 1   A Dutch woman, held as a spy

2   Belgian man, friend of woman
3   An Italian ... Saboteur
4   A Bosch Soldier

What a collection! Return to Sulmona with Iti in Fiat. Cpl Guther arrives with other two. All locked up in the jail for the night. Had a lovely hot bath at 6.00pm! Several ex POWs arrive – Place seething with Ities wanting for this that and the other! Went to have dinner with an American Ex POW who had been living with civilians in Sulmona for 9 months in hiding. He had been shot down in a fortress over Catania in Sicily.

Had a most <u>enormous</u> dinner – lasted 3½ hours; about 10 courses including liqueurs, vino, strawberries etc. Back in house by 11.00pm.

Seventeen miles away the less fortunate citizens of Palena are entering and trying, as Shaw reports, to make the best of their wrecked houses. A Squadron now comes back into Palena, into the bivouac area, as the rest of 1HCR regroups having been informed they will move out of the area on June 17, 177 miles to Castel Nova and return to its mobile role. 'The many lessons learned during the past few weeks have been extremely useful,' comments the Adjutant in his official report, 'as at any time the Regiment may again be ordered to operate in a dismounted role.'

***

They are up very early for the new move south-east, their route taking them through Alessa, Assisi, Castiglione, Carpinove, Vinchiatarci, Volturara to one of the many villages or towns called Castel Nova overlooking the plain of Foggia. In their Daimlers and Staghounds, their White scout cars, their Dingos, the three tonners and other vehicles – nearly 200 in all – they make an impressive column rolling through towns and villages, greeted by cheers and garlands from the war-weary but now liberated populace.

They are not happy; they are warriors returning to idle time away in camp, as they did at Sidi Bishr, near Cairo. Ewart complains they have too much of an easy time. 'All they do is grumble,' he writes. 'They will certainly have to improve soon or something will be done about it ... One learns the value of drill more and more and I think it would not be a bad idea if I have drill every day.'

Shaw is more sanguine and relishes the respite before more action. He is fed up with the unseasonable high wind and heavy rain – they are near the Adriatic. The cherries in season are delicious, while he and Valerian find some 'quite good' local wine. Valerian has a bad leg, so Shaw is temporarily 2i/c but a few days later they and Fraser go pigeon shooting in the fields.

Now it is exercise time again, and they are joined by a new draft of nearly 100 men, forming four Squadrons instead of three, each of approximately 150 men, with another 156 making up the Regimental and Headquarters Squadron. The officers are fairly comfortable: 'Dug my bivvy in very well and should be pretty comfortable,' says Shaw, and they have a nice house where 55 officers mess; but the torrential rain goes on. 'Pity the rest of the Regiment in the fields.' Manoeuvres occupy them for the last fortnight in June. Then the sun comes out on the three squadrons advancing to the sea near Bari, opposed by a skeletal force in 'Exercise Agrippa'. Between times they swim and sunbathe, camping 200 yards from the sea under almond trees.

Bari, a huge centre of allied supplies, was badly hit in December 1943 when Junkers Ju88 successfully bombed the harbour, destroying ships including the US Liberty vessel *John Harvey* whose cargo was mustard gas to counter possible German use. As a result, as many as 1,000 servicemen and 1,000 Italians died from the 'immersion and exposure' to the gas. This set-back is called 'Little Pearl Harbor' – a catastrophe that was first hushed up, then later covered up.

In the second week of July they are mounted en route for the line again, moving up the route the 5th Army have taken to pursue the Germans. This logistic task is entrusted to Henry Uxbridge, the transport officer. It becomes the highlight, he says, of his career: his recent recollection may be hazy and underestimate the numbers:

Most important moment in my life – The Colonel said, 'You, Henry, are to be in charge of the great changeover.' On the left of Italy was one corps and on the other there was another. 'You have to transfer us from east to west. Henry, you have two months to organize this. 23 or 24 small cars – Daimlers – with 5 men in them. All the roads have to be slightly "amended" to start with, and secondly there will be all sort of difficulties getting through villages.' Anyway I was put in charge.

On July 9 Shaw passed through the desolation of Cassino, and on through Rome to a staging camp at Guita Costellana. 'A most interesting and beautiful drive. The work of the RAF well illustrated by the wrecks on the road side.' Ewart:

> Drove through Rome – not particularly impressed as did not go anywhere near the interesting parts. Saw Cassino and some of the tanks etc that had been knocked off. Cassino really was the most amazing sight – completely demolished. It is a marvel how anyone ever captured Monastery Hill.

And now they are back in action, ranged or spread out south of Perugia with the enemy retreating before them, their old antagonists the Austrian mountain troops (85th Mt Regiment) in a fast and fluid war. They are allotted to so many different formations successively that, as Herbert recalls, it would be tedious to name them all. But as part of the Habforce taking over from the Carpathian Lancers under the command known as 2 Pole Corps, the veterans of the storming of Monte Cassino (the 12th and 15th Polish Lancers) they face an enemy superior in numbers. Their job is to pursue relentlessly, hampered by road craters, mines, booby traps and well positioned artillery and mortar fire.

There is some trouble, too, with the roving, aggressive tactics of the Polish 'Popski's Private Army', whose units they shell by mistake, causing no casualties but provoking considerable indignation from Popski himself, Colonel Vladimir Peniakov. This phase is long and hard, constantly mobile and dangerous as the fluid German line recedes into well fortified positions, known as the Gothic Line. Ewart:

> *Sunday July 16.* Went to Mass in morning at 10 in a little village called Santo Marino where the Germans had been to Mass the week before. It was very odd doing this ...
>
> During afternoon very odd things happened. Teddy asked to do something and he was told that he could not and he proceeded to have a very long argument over the air about it. Eventually it was reported that he had hit a mine and had turned completely over. Luckily no one was hurt. He got back very late, we waited till about 9 before going into leaguer.

This is a new, tough phase, as they suffer more casualties and lose vehicles. Shaw, unhurt, with his troop lifts a lot of mines, and the Regiment is now containing the major part of a German division on a 20-mile front. Ewart:

Saturday. Went on patrol about 11am just behind Donato. Fired spasmodically all day. In evening we were in middle of our brew and we had to fire again. I went off in dingo to our O.P. All of a sudden a shell landed some way away from me and Marston's voice was shouting over the air, 'They're ranging on us!' Went down and things were a bit chaotic but I began to try and put things right. The next shell that landed fell next door to one of the Whites and hit Ovenden's. He screamed very loudly and ran towards me. Took him into the house with Marston and Lambert and saw the White [half-track scout car] disappear in a cloud of dust. Ovenden's arm looked ghastly and we waited in the house whilst they were shelling the place. I had my doubts as to whether we would survive or not. Eventually it ended and things got straightened out a bit. Never been so frightened in my life. This night I shall sleep. It was the nearest miss of near misses.

The chase continues to the north of Arezzo, some 15 miles south-east of Florence, but at the end of a week of fast pursuit action moving north, A Squadron is pulled back. Du Plessis:

This method of locating and keeping contact with a retreating enemy is simple and effective but after a time it is necessary to pull back and re-equip the forward troops in men or materials, and sometimes even give them a rest so that they can catch up with some sleep and give their tattered nerves a chance to unwind. It was in just such a period of disengagement that A Squadron found itself quartered on a pleasant stretch of farmland somewhere just South of Florence. In such cases our Second in Command Valerian had the thankless task of approaching the owner and informing him or her courteously but firmly that fifty-odd wheeled and tracked armoured vehicles would be dispersing themselves over their growing cornfields. On this particular property Valerian met with friendliness and cooperation and the farm in question was not all down to corn but had many pastures, orchards, poultry yards, vines, barns and sheds, with fallow sections where we were able to spread ourselves out without doing any damage to crops. Freeman set up my personal little bivouac in a hazel grove on the edge of a bubbling stream. That was close to paradise itself!

151

Valerian extended an invitation to supper to the lady of the house and her husband and on such occasions our mess waiter, Corporal Stead, was usually able to pool all our individual tins of stew into one big dish, accompanied by a mountain of boiled potatoes; I cannot for the life of me remember one single pudding beyond tinned peach halves or pears with Bird's custard. Our guests politely gave the impression that they were tasting nectar and reciprocally asked us to dine with them on the morrow in the big house. This hospitality was repeated more than once.

Food was short in those days even on a farm and discreetly we decided to limit our numbers to five when we went up, taking it in turns, because the family itself numbered at least five if not six. They were I believe called Boncompagni; there was one grown-up daughter named Imperia and one daughter-in-law. We sat down to a big dining table laid for about ten or twelve people. Usually I sat on one side of our hostess acting as interpreter: my Italianised French was not elegant but it was better than nothing and we managed some sort of conversation. I think the property belonged to her, our hostess, rather than to her husband, or perhaps it belonged to her old father who sat at the other end of the table, reminiscing about great shooting parties he had held there in happier times, evaluating their success by the number of quintals of pasta and litres of wine consumed. Normally the family lived in Bologna which was still occupied, and meanwhile they stayed on this, their country property, glad to be on the 'free' side.

Sometimes after dinner we would be invited to have coffee with them, (wartime coffee made of burnt wheat or whatever: every family had a secret recipe) sitting outside under the canopy of a starlit summer night, Florence just visible in the distance. Valerian tried to repay their hospitality by sending up what we could spare of such things as tea, Nescafe, tinned beef, and cigarettes. These things were precious and were appreciated. Sometimes we would bring a bottle of whisky with us. We became real friends.

The day of departure came but for security reasons we couldn't give them much notice. We said our goodbyes the evening before, after coffee. The next morning while we were preparing and loading our cars, we received from them the most extraordinary present. A young woman arrived from the farm bearing under her arm a varnished wicker basket in which sat a young goose with a red ribbon round its neck. The goose sat calmly in her basket, her upper half immaculately white. The woman put the basket down, smilingly saying something like: 'La Signora asked me to give you this young goose. We wish you a safe journey. God be with you.' And she withdrew, leaving us speechless.

That the goose was intended for the pot there was no doubt; in any other country it would have arrived upside down, legs trussed, head bent back and protesting loudly. But that is not the Italian way: their sense of style required that this young goose should be presented to us in all her natural beauty, with a ribbon round her neck. To us though she was something young and innocent in need of protection and love. She would be our pet, that was an instant, if mute decision.

During this respite, Valerian sets off in a jeep with some men on an expedition of his own.

It was a tiresome time because of the roads and no one could step off the roads into verges – culverts were blown up we had a few brushes with the enemy. We halted on the eastern outskirts of Florence. Our instructions were not to go in. High level discussions were happening in Switzerland with the Germans not to blow the Ponte Vecchio. They had blown up all the other bridges.

After three days Eric Gooch was getting very impatient. He said, Could I sneak in with a jeep and three men and find out what was going on? This made us the first Allied soldiers to enter Florence. We got to a charming square with masses of people who were delighted to see us, all sorts of exciting prospects, beautiful girls throwing garlands around our necks – that sort of thing. I was given a frightfully good, very boozy lunch by a rather grand family. I had no papers on me of course. They produced an old set of cards and we wrote our names on them.

I got good intelligence that the Germans were over the Ponte Vecchio still in the north of Florence, but I had no contact with them. Then we were sat outside Florence for three more days. A brave young officer, Lt Robin Tudsbery, went out and captured fifteen Germans, killed two or three. Gathered a lot of info. He got a Military Cross but sadly was killed a week before the end of the war – blown up in his armoured car by a naval mine lodged under a culvert – nice chap.

We then marched in with the 51st Highland Division with their pipes playing. Soon after that we left there and went straight to Rimini on the east coast where the Germans were withdrawing very fast. As we knew before we left, I told my wife – she was still in Jerusalem working on military intelligence – I told her to keep an eye on the operations map as she had access to it. We had no wireless contact, and were not allowed to mention where we were. I wrote her a letter once a week. Anyway, I said, when you see we're going to return to England for god's sake get yourself on to a ship home. This she did.

The Regimental goose has been spared, du Plessis tells us, with the ease of a natural story-teller:

Time was against us. Engines were being started and warmed up, radio operators were tuning into their control frequencies, the last bedrolls were being strapped atop their designated mudguards. This was one aspect of active service in which armoured regiments were luckier than many others: each member of a three-man crew was assured of a place for his bedroll on his own vehicle's mudguards, a large flat affair on top of each wheel; and the fourth wheel-top was available for general purposes, whatever these might be. Our goose was quickly allocated to general purposes and Trooper Freeman, who was to be her most active foster parent, secured the basket firmly to the free wheel-top, having already crisscrossed a webbing strap from side to side of the basket-top, so that its occupant could neither stand up nor open out her wings. She seemed very placid and compliant. She must have been used to being handled.

So we moved off, an impressive sight with our engines roaring, pennants flying, car-commanders atop their open turrets with a loud-speaker in one hand and headphones adjusted over their berets. Our Italian friends of all grades were there to gape and in some cases wave to the men they had come to know as friends during a brief but close acquaintance. And our goose drew her share of attention: 'La Occa, La Occa!' they cried out and pointed with delight when they saw her, proud and serene in her red ribbon.

At our journey's end, when our time became our own, Freeman tied a long cord to the red ribbon and he let his goose graze and wander. She seemed quite tame. To supplement her diet of roadside grass she got a mugful of porridge oats mixed with a little water; she seemed to enjoy that and as porridge was not a priority with us crushed oats became a part of her daily ration and she thrived on them.

Towards the end of this spell in the first weeks of August, it seemed to Ewart A Squadron was going into reserve. He meets Porchey again, and hears Porchey's old servant, Steel, has been killed. Meantime, Porchey writing home to his father and mother is not at all enamoured of the heat, the flies, the rain – or the Italians. Earlier from Bari he has written, 'This might be such a pleasant country, spoilt by its inhabitants, I hate them, filthy dirty people, although some are grand fighters among the partisans. We have had experience of them. The German atrocities to women in the villages were ghastly and don't bear repeating, no wonder their husbands and lovers fight hard and ask no quarter.'

The father-son preoccupation with Pups' second wife surfaces again as Porchey asks for news of Tilly, and Carnarvon replies: 'Bad news from USA regarding Tilly, as she has got the cheek to <u>defend</u> her case and that will delay everything terribly. Jeanne [Porchey's sister] is well and sends love, as do Sydney and Heidy who are now at Highclere ... Tilly's excuse so far is that she states she is in America with my full consent! If that is the best she can do, her fate seems about the same as Hitler's!' Porchey, in answer to his further concerns, hears more about Tilly:

> There is not much news from the Tilly front, except that she had to change her solicitors and is now being represented by a firm of people in Canada, whose London agent is named Oppenheimer, which sounds to me rather ominous, and maybe they found out that she was not a very good partner! I have since discovered that she owes £900 to some solicitors who represented her in her previous divorce case, and who are still screaming for their account to be settled. I have passed on this titbit of news to the people who are acting for her now, so that they should not be caught unawares, and if there is anything of a trade union movement in their profession she ought soon to find it quite difficult to get people to work for her!

Porchey is lunching with Tilly's friend, Cecil Beaton, on October 2. Beaton has seen Tilly and 'I expect will make some interesting proposition on her behalf ...' Since the loss of Steel, his servant, Porchey has taken over Hennings, Gavin Astor's servant, as his own.

Porchey's friend Ewart, in charge of the 75mm battery, confides to his diary as usual in a way the others do not:

August 8. Did not get much sleep last night so pleased to come into squadron area this morning. It gets terribly close in the night and it was a most unpleasant business getting up – dirty and damp. All the Jerries dispersed this morning but later heard they were all coming back. Again this was cancelled thank goodness. I don't think I mind being in same troop as D or B but not in C.

Went back to position and spent peaceful morning washing or talking more accurately getting laundry ready, airing and making a bed. By the time this was done it was time for lunch. After lunch slept – but forgot to make allowance for the sun and found myself in the boiling heat instead of the shade. I cannot stand the naked sun – it almost drives me mad. The worst part of this sort of life is the bloody diarrhoea which at the moment is playing hell with me. It makes me feel quite ill. Anyhow the war is obviously ending soon and then home.

CHAPTER FOURTEEN

U.S. SANGRI-LA VERSUS A SQUADRON RHG

All enjoy the warmth that accompanies boasting, the fierce electric thrill of hatred. Some take pleasure in the act of fighting. But none enjoy (though it is extraordinary how many are ready stoically to bear) starvation, wounds, and violent death.

Aldous Huxley, *Stories, Essays and Poems* (quoted by Van Ammel in his Oflag 79 log-book)

The war is not ending. It is August 1944 and there are still eight months, and many, many thousands of casualties down the line. The mismanaged capitulation of Italy, its changing sides and the speedy exploitation of the Italian situation by the Nazis, logistic and armament production, above all its skilled and professional armies in the face of superior Allied air and army forces, led by tactically brilliant commanders, keep the Germans in the fight.

Much is talked of the evil of Hitler and the theory of the master-race. I sometimes wonder if just as real an evil at this time, as well as her Führer's madness, was Germany's self-perpetuating, huge industrial capacity and the North European work ethic that sucked in the German people to single-minded production. Ultimately either brainwashed, or brutally, even skilfully, disciplined, people are being sacrificed to 'output' – her machines, her scientific prowess, and her technical superiority. In this it may be that the Promethean genius of Albert Speer is just as culpable, in terms of the body count he causes, as the Führer's genocidal henchmen. Speer, playing Mephistopheles to Hitler, fed his creative imagination, his dreams of everlasting glory, architectural wonders, of ultimate godlike control, with his own practical skills and manpower management. An overlooked part of Hitler's extraordinary power was his perception in picking the right men to realise his messianic vision: we should remember his alleged last words: 'Here dies a great artist ...'

The skilful delaying retreat from Italy, strategically executed by Kesselring, was crucial to that extra year of Third Reich glory in defeat enjoyed by the megalomaniac holding on to power, and the heavily fuelled determination of the armed forces to avoid humiliation at all costs.

As the Nazi empire shrunk, Speer cranked up output: 'Advised the Führer once more on the importance of Italian armament and war production and informed him that about 15% of the German armaments volume will drop off if Italy produces no more for us. The Führer emphasises that the importance is clear to him.' During a speech a month later, Speer reminded his audience that German war production depended upon the Italian and Western European economies for 25 to 30% of output. Moreover, purchases of essential goods from Italy between April 17 and October 10, 1944 had climbed to RM 299,000,000. Despite aerial bombardment, labour unrest and raw material shortages, Italy played an invaluable role in replacing production lost in the East and elsewhere in the West throughout 1944.

So Italy's industrial production is still being diverted even in the summer of 1944 – chemicals, cloth, metals – and its 1944 harvest replaces foodstuff lost from Russian, Polish and Romanian farms,. Above all, Italian skilled manpower aids the German war effort. At the Nuremburg trials Speer is to testify: 'In 1944 seven times as many weapons were manufactured as in 1942, five-and-a-half times as many armoured vehicles, and six times as much ammunition. The number of workers in these branches increased only by 30%. This success was not brought about through a greater exploitation of labour but rather through the abolition of obsolete methods of production and through an improved system.'

Field Marshal Alexander's blithe assumption that the retreating German divisions would collapse shows delusions can be shared on both sides, while his blindness to the technical advantages offered to the defender by mountainous terrain is reflected in the continual attrition of Allied numbers lost in forgotten battles.

A particular example of the folly of war is the confusion of higher command over the advancing 1HCR. There are now men from 28 or 29 nations fighting the Germans. On August 3 a piano fell on the jeep carrying General Templar, the Allied Commander, from a passing lorry, and his injury made him relinquish control. Indecision in the higher ranks of the 8th Army means that in 24 hours the Regiment is under the command of three different corps: at 1800 hours on the 11th they passed from 6th Armoured Division to 13 Corps; from 0200 to 1100 hours on the 12th they were under 10 Corps; and after that under Polish II Corps. Translating this into A Squadron activity, Fraser notes:

> ... Warning order to move shortly at 12.00 noon. Maddening! We are to go back to right sector under Polish Corps!! Pack up kit in evening and move out onto track for night ready to leave tomorrow morning.

> *Saturday August 12.* Rev 0300hrs. Move out at 3.20am for the start point. Very narrow track and very dark. Have about 10 mins to get breakfast. Cross SP at 6.20am. Route Arezzo, Perugia and route 77 to Murcia and Matelica. First halt at 4.30pm. Total 200 miles in 19 hrs. Very bad to start, getting better later. Thick dust everywhere. Get in 10pm. Very tired and dirty. League short of Jesi A and B Sqns are going up again shortly – A Sqn again.

The usual meticulous Ewart records the discrepancies in their orders and points to an underlying uncertainty in this new combat zone on the Gothic Line, where a new pattern of pricking and probing enemy positions will become established.

> Reveille was at 0315 this morning and we drove practically all day till 11pm at night. We were originally going to Nouova to join a force of 9th Armoured Brigade, 27th and 12th Lancers. However as we got into Perugia the order was changed and we were told to go to Jesi to join the Polish Corps. The whole Regiment went the wrong way and it was all rather chaotic. Went via Arezzo Perugia, Foliglio, Jesi.

Hearing the armies in France are 30 miles from Paris his heart leaps with hope that he will be home by Christmas, but the discomforts of their concentration area just behind the front means 'practically every car gets bogged'. The flies are terrible and the smells where he is billeted are atrocious. A few days later he fears he is getting malaria.

The more sanguine Shaw, now promoted to Captain, and Liaison Officer with the Poles:

Saturday August 12. Set off very early in the morning after breakfast at 0300. Saw the regt started and set off to 10 corps with the col and arranged everything there. Went on to catch up the regiment. No signs of them at Nocera, so went on to Foligno, where we met C of H Gibbons who said the regt had now been told to go to Jesi and come under Polcorps. Went on to catch them up found them blocking the road completely in Senna Valle. Colonel very annoyed, luckily chaos soon sorted out.

I am sent on to Jesi to recce new area. Did so and had dinner with Poles at CIZ. Regt however moved into different areas to mine. Didn't get to bed til 0230.

Sunday August 13. Up early putting vehicles in places of better camouflage. Kept busy on small jobs around the camp most of the day. Went to Polecorp and near Corps with Leo in the evening.

We are going to join a Cavalry Group with the 12 and 15 Polish Lancers, the Carpathian Lancers and the 7 HAR sound quite fun. The whole commanded by Gen S. Csysko-Bohusz.

Skirmishes and casualties apart – those for the Regiment are as heavy as ever – they are socially busy. They have alongside them a brigade or large group of Italian partisans, the Maiella Brigade, from the Monte Amaro area. They are to relieve it. The night before this takeover they discover the Italian artillery officer they are dining with commanded a battery exactly opposite 1HCR at the battle of Alamein. During this dinner, at a sudden outburst of small arms fire, Gooch jumps to his feet. 'Is that an enemy patrol?' he demands of the Italian Brigade Commander. 'Rest assured – just my men celebrating that they are coming out of the line.'

In direct confrontation once again with the enemy, daily patrols are mounted. Their forward positions are shelled and mortared. It does not surprise, given their now well-honed skills of survival, that in 30 minutes on August 21, roughly 250 shells fall on B Squadron inflicting no casualties. The profligacy of war.

Their Polish comrades-in-arms are much enjoyed by the Regiment's officers. Uxbridge:

> So His Majesty's Royal troops were put under the Poles. The only surprising thing that happened was I met General Anders personally. He was a wonderful man. We later wore on our battle dress the battle honour of Warsaw.
>
> They were really fascinating, the Poles. The other ranks were extraordinary because although when we first arrived they were out of the line, they would go forward one by one by themselves at night to see if they could kill a German. This is actual fact, and they came back quite often with a corpse – extraordinary! The Polish officers all spoke perfect English. They ... were waiting to get at the Russians in due course!
>
> I can tell you that our troops were tremendously impressed by how good the Poles were and I may say the officers got on with them perfectly well and we all seemed to stand around making conversation on the east coast before we somehow got forward. That was one of my most fascinating times. We did not get far up the right of Italy, but we began to get a bit of trouble with the enemy.

As far as I can tell, Henry Uxbridge is the only one of these officers who actually confesses to killing a German. Earlier he had on two occasions 'gone up a hill to see if I could attack some Germans. I was very lucky because I found one on skis and I shot at him and killed him, and brought him back. The only time I was ever at all a real soldier!'

John Shaw is liaising well, too, with the Poles, an essential part of which is dinner:

> In the evening Nigel and myself went over to the Karp Lancers again for dinner. Big party there with Col Sarkrewski, the Col, and the General, and Col Mokrzycki the G1. Very good dinner and a lot to drink. Drinking, talking, and singing until very late. Very amusing until 1230 when I got very fixed and eventually fell asleep. Don't think anyone was over-annoyed though.
>
> *Thursday August 17.* Somewhat of a row with Mokrzycki in the morning over the lateness of the regt. However I think it was mainly from the night before. General Anders and some American General who is Deputy

Chief of Staff AA1 came to lunch and in consequence a very good lunch was had by all. I had to sit at the top table and talk a good deal with the American – not a very exciting man, rather dumb.

Meanwhile, what is happening to the gift from the grateful Italians entrusted to Herbert?

Northwards from Florence to the Gothic Line where the Germans turned at bay and stood their ground, our goose shared our life, completely tame. During periods of rest or maintenance she wandered free between the cars while the men attended to their engines, guns, wireless sets or whatever. Sometimes she liked to play the fool: she would do a sort of half pirouette on one leg, then on the other, making strange little honking noises. Pure attention seeking no doubt! At night while we slept, each one of us with his head against a wheel, she would be shut inside the car in her basket so as to be safe from any harm. And all was for the best in the best of all possible worlds for our little goose until the day of the boxing match.

One of the 'rests' A Squadron enjoy is in Sassoferato, a small town where Tony the Squadron commander pushes Herbert to organise games to entertain the men. Du Plessis:

I have in my possession a piece of red silk done up at the top into a rosette, from which hangs a sort of tasseled banner with a gold threaded inscription as follows:

U.S. Sangri-La

V

A Squadron

R.H.G.

The initials 'U.S.' have nothing to do with our friends and allies the Yanks. They stand for the words: 'Unique Sportiva' Sangri-La.

I went to see the mayor and asked if he would be interested in promoting a football match. He smiled wryly: '*Tenente*,' he said 'have you seen our football ground? You could not walk across it for shell holes.' But he wanted to help. His own townspeople were as much in need of

162

a morale boost as we were. Food was short, and the town had suffered terribly from bombing and shelling; the power lines were down and no one could say when electricity would be restored. Now this war which they had never wanted was ravaging their lovely homeland. The only blessing was that for them, in this town, it was all over; but what prospects did they have? Where would food and work be coming from? Life must have been grim.

The mayor introduced me to the secretary of their sporting club whom we shall call Mario to fill the gap in my memory. 'What about boxing?' he said. Boxing! In the two years that I had been with the Regiment in the Middle East and onwards there had been no such thing and all I knew was that there were indeed some boxers about in A Squadron; but it was all from talk; and our Regimental champion Trooper Hislop was now somewhere in a hospital at base probably minus a leg for all I knew.

What weights could we match? The sport was so deeply anchored in its English origins that we had no difficulty putting down the English names of the categories and their weight limits in Imperial stones and pounds, to which Mario counter-matched his kilos. To make a match we would need to offer, say, eight contests in the different weights but as we might be short of men in the very lightest categories we would offer more than one contest in middling categories. So we agreed on a match in categories as follows (all weights in Imperial lbs, being the maximum permitted for each category): Bantam (112lbs) Feather (125) Light (132) Welter (147) Light/Middle (156) and Light/Heavyweight (178). As Mario had no Light/Heavyweights he offered to box himself, a middleweight, against me, at Light-Heavyweight, conceding about a stone; but such a contest could not count in the formal results and would be classed as an 'exhibition match' which means that the contestants box normally but stop short of a knock-out, if the opponent is hurt. The normal procedure then is to mess about in a clinch until it is safe to let go.

Mario and the Mayor were so keen to set up the match that they took on the hundred-and-one arrangements that go into a public contest: lending us gloves, building a ring, which they did in the Town Hall with ample seating; providing lighting which came from a huge brown generator activated by a massive traction engine of early nineteen hundreds vintage; they provided scales for the boxers to be weighed; a time-keeper and a referee (we must have offered a counterpart but I can't remember who) and I believe we asked our own doctor, Leo Lonsdale, the Regimental

M.O., to attend. I didn't have much to do except take my chaps jogging because boxers, like dancers, need legs.

The day of the event came (at the end of a week) and I was surprised and elated by the feverish queuing for seats among the townspeople; I had reserved a generous section for our own Squadron. The interior of the Town Hall was beautifully presented. An imposing ring stood proud on a dais, a blaze of lights was focused upon it, the seats were full, there was a buzz of anticipation in the air. We had seen nothing like this in a long time and nor had the townspeople. I took my place as chief second in 'the Red corner' where there was a bucket of water, a towel and a sponge ready and waiting. Mario had thought of all the details! The Bantams of each team arrived and took their seat on the stool. 'Seconds out!' said the referee, and the bell clanged: the fight was on.

To our dismay things went wrong from the start: our first man was flat on his back in no time at all. Our second man, at Lightweight, did not fare much better and was obviously bested on points. You could feel rather than hear the excitement in the Italian ranks, who were too polite to cheer derisively at the discomfiture of the challenging nation which until a few months back had been an enemy. Their behaviour was impeccable but our dismay was palpable.

We had to wait for the third contest at least before the honours began to be shared evenly. The middling weights went mostly our way. At last it came to be my turn to climb into the ring as a contestant and to face Mario across the ring. He was a handsome man, with closely clipped black hair framing a fine forehead and regular features. He was a stone lighter than me but an expert boxer. He adopted the square footed American stance, face guarded equally with both gloves, ready to attack with either hand on demand and very fast. We fought three hard and quite painful rounds with no decision given as it was an 'exhibition' but I have no doubt that he was getting the better of me in the third round. After the event my driver Trooper `Hudson gave me his verdict: 'You done all right, Sir, it was an even fight but we could see you was suffering at the end.' However there was a lot of cheering when the fight came to an end, not just for us the last contestants but at the whole event which was appreciated by British and Italians alike.

The contest could be called a draw but for the Italians it must have had the flavour of redemption: these people had spent years rather than months watching their troops being repulsed and beaten everywhere, first losing their sometime empire in East Africa, where they surrendered a whole army and its men and materials to the British; then being pushed by them across the North face of Libya, into Tunisia where the British 8th Army met the newly arrived Americans; losing Sicily to the Allies, with never a redeeming victory in all this; and finally capitulating and being treated like a subjected people by their erstwhile allies the Germans, who ravaged their country at will while they laid it waste to hamper the Allied invasion of Italy itself. Now in this boxing contest they had stood man to man facing the English conqueror and proved that on equal terms they also could be brave and take punishment and win as many contests as they lost. It was a happy and noisy crowd that filed out of the Town Hall, elated at the 'divertimento'.

I went to find Mario. I asked him if he would kindly let me keep the fine length of red silk which we in 'the Red corner' had worn around our waist while we gave battle. He said that he would recover it and bring it to me at my car. Two days passed and just when I had begun to think that Mario had forgotten he appeared with it in his hand, but now fashioned into the banner which I have described. The initials R.H.G. he took from the shoulder flashes on my battledress: Royal Horse Guards. It would have been more correct to put: H.C.R. But he wanted to surprise me.

Sangri-La? I had heard a radio play a few years before the War when I was perhaps fourteen years old and it had made a deep impression on me. I did not know then as I know now that the origin of the play was a best-selling novel by James Hilton, *Lost Horizon*, published in 1933 and featuring a mysterious earthly paradise in the Himalayas named Shangri-La. How amazing that this English fantasy had struck such a chord abroad as to be adopted for its name by a provincial Italian sporting club. No doubt the connotation was that in sport one could escape all the pressures and the corruptive influence of modern life to attain an ideal, not only of physical wellbeing but also of a perfect relationship with one's fellow men. Mario was the epitome of that ideal.

I had rarely seen Tony so obviously pleased by something his Squadron had done. But our elation at the success of the boxing match was marred by an incident at the end of that day.

The match had finished in the late afternoon and when we returned to our cars someone said: 'Where is the goose?' Where indeed? We looked about us and then at each other and after a time we had to admit that she had gone. Whose fault was it? Perhaps we were all guilty that in our absorption by the impending boxing match we had forgotten about her. Would some passer-by have snatched her? Hardly likely; grabbing a full grown goose would have been a noisy business drawing a lot of attention. Or had the Thirty Pieces of Silver played their insidious part? Her going left an aura of guilt, sadness and suspicion which persisted for quite a few days.

The sequel to this is probably – and sadly – recorded in Fraser's diary (August 23) when he comments on how good the Poles are. Two of them, on either side of him, are having eggs for breakfast and lunch. Then he writes, 'Have a goose for dinner.'

CHAPTER FIFTEEN

THE LAST BATTLE

The cannon had ceased to roar and silence had sunk on the land. The ground before me was a quagmire and, if a man took a fall he rose with a coat of mud from head to foot. The horses were in no better case. I soon saw the Regiment coming back, so covered with black mud that their faces were hardly distinguishable and the colour of their scarlet uniforms invisible.

Assistant Surgeon Haddy James, Life Guards, 1815

Most of the rest of August is taken up crossing and protecting rivers in the mountainous area to the south of the resort of Axis-held Pesaro, which is the Adriatic end of the Gothic Line. They are 3 miles south of Pesaro. Although the conditions are bad and they suffer casualties from mines and continuous heavy shelling from German artillery on higher ground, which is well ranged on road crossings, all units coordinate well in this work:

W.O. Diary. 0700 Lieut. K.W.D. Diacre's Armd C Tp crossed the river, going extremely slow owing to innumerable mines chiefly Box and Schumines although some 250lb aerial bombs were encountered being used as ground mines. Det Pol Eng (95) gave invaluable assistance lifting these mines.

An insight into Gooch's command style is supplied by the Polish liaison officer, Captain Mantel: 'The HQ was always in the open, for Gooch cares more for the beauty than the utility of his surroundings, which he declares greatly influence and contribute to the success of his work ... [Now it is] in the open under the poplar trees, though close at hand was a lovely villa. Villa Milani and its hospitable owner has offered us quarters, the use of the bathrooms, wine and even macaroni.'

Meantime Lt-Col Andrew Ferguson arrives from England to visit the Regiment for 48 hours. A bridge over the Mataura River on the approach to Pesaro is blown by Polish Sappers despite heavy shelling. Then Diacre's leading Dingo is blown up on a mine and two men injured. On August 29:

Pol Engineers failed to complete the br over the canal until 1200hrs when D Sqn passed two tps over it, thence over the Arzilla by crossing at S/738. One Tp under Lieut. Hon. R.E.J.R. Watson went right to try and move up main coast rd but held up by mines. The left tp under Lieut. G.E. Noble moved North and made contact at S/792 just before last night. B Sqn Carp L were adv down same axis as D Sqn, which did not improve the situation for either sqn. At last light D Sqn held a line from S/780 t S/763. RHQ moved up to S/737 before last light. Coy Banda di Patriote di Maiella under comd Regt.

At first light D Sqn tps moved fwd and entered Pesaro at 1000hrs. B Sqn Carp L entered the town same time.

1030 Two Armed C Tps and Sp Tp D Sqn in the town in contact with the enemy who shelled the town heavily. CO ordered C Sqn up just South of Pesaro to be prepared to assist D Sqn. B Sqn Carp L also in town and as co-operation with Carp L became impossible CO ordered D Sqn to withdraw to OPs South of the town. Lieut. G.E. Noble, CofH Craddock and six men wounded, Tprs Hard and Wanstall killed in the town. The enemy continued to shell the town and the South exits throughout the day.

1700 Carp L withdrew from the town. CO ordered C Sqn to take over from D Sqn at last light covering the Southern entrances to the town. RHQ moved up to S/736.

August 31. During the morning C Sqn remained in observation of Pesaro, enemy shelled spasmodically. At 1230 hrs CO ordered Lieut. J.W.A. Greenish and Lieut. E.G. Lambton's Tps with two pls Banda Maiella under comd to dv into the town but not to become involved. The centre of the town was reached with no contact but enemy put two heavy stonks down behind this party which was thought possibly to be the preliminary of an attempt to cut them off, so were ordered to withdraw. Later enemy were seen in the North East part of the town and contact was made by Carp L on the West.

The War Office Diary entries, admirably succinct, give an indication of the ebb and flow of movement.

Captain Mantel reports how active the Household Cavalry is on the right of the Polish II Corps, and there begins a race between the two, which favours the Polish vehicles, although the road is heavily mined. Along Highway 16 the HCR are winning, managing to get to Fano first, after crossing the Metauro. Mantel:

> But, as soon as we got over, our riders made full use of their spurs and made a perfect run to Pesaro. The liaison officers had the biggest thrill from the race. Our liaison officer returned to HQ. H.R. Regt with the map references of our patrols, but as tea was being served had to possess himself in patience. Immediately tea was over, he informed Lt. Col. Gooch of the position on our sector. Our patrols were actually ahead of those of the H.C. Regt and were pushing hard on to Pesaro. Lt. Col. Gooch took up his mike and called up his squadron leader and shouted his famous 'Push on, Push on – Lobsters ahead!' At the time our liaison officer didn't know what on earth he was talking about, and it was not until later that he learnt that Pesaro was noted for its delicious lobsters.

Both patrols arrive in a dead heat and become inextricably mixed up, fighting shoulder to shoulder.

While Fraser and his troop are guarding A Squadron HQ, the other squadrons are moving into the suburbs of Pesaro. Some of D Squadron enter the town where 300 men of the 1st German Parachute Division are dug in; but a Polish Carpathian Squadron is also there. Fortunately, a German prisoner taken by the Poles breaks under interrogation, revealing the paratroops are going to encircle the HCR troop under Diacre, and when C Squadron enters the town next day it finds an artillery barrage put down behind it. Fearing a counter-attack and then being cut off, Gooch orders withdrawal.

Meanwhile Ewart, who has the gun troop, has a problem: he finds some of his troop are drinking too much and has to put an end to it. He feels it is the only way 'to control things. Very bitter feelings all round.

I got no thanks for my pains.' Tony Murray-Smith speaks to him after this and he tells Ewart some disturbing news, that the Colonel has received a telegram from Colonel Andrew about his father, who has a brain tumour. In the midst of engagement the news of his father's illness unsettles him and he wants to leave Italy at once to be with him and help in his father's business:

Daddy was undergoing serious operation and he [Ferguson] would send another telegram in 3 days time. News rather took me aback but I hope I did not show it. The two above incidents made me feel very browned off with life. Then went to OP and did some shooting. For some reason I could not see the shots land and it was an unsuccessful day on the whole. Everyone of the 96th Div. has been up here and it has been a very lousy place. This evening we were shelled quite heavily but we buoyed well up and no one was hurt. In evening went back to squadron where I got telegram from Mummy saying that Daddy had undergone successful operation for tumour on the brain. That is a great relief. I hope he is quite all right. This morning we began maintenance in earnest. Lambert [Ewart's servant] phoned Squadron leader again. I approached Tony about my bid to take over 2nd troop and have Hudson take guns. Am not certain ditching them will come off yet but hope it will. It will occupy me and will make the most of a bad job.

This evening got Mummy's first letters about Daddy. If things go badly I will definitely have to get home and to take over. After conference Tony tells me that I have got to keep 1 troop. Rather disappointed, especially as Ford goes to drive Tony and Hopkins to operate Corporal Hope's car. I get Williams and Humphries instead. Heard that regiment will soon be withdrawn – until the door opens into Plains of Lombardy.

He is finding this such a whirlwind of events that it is difficult for him to keep focused on the work in hand, and he strives, without success, to give up command of the Heavy Troop.

The 7th Lancers and the Regiment again enjoy the cavalry rivalry in action, and party together: one such is held at Ostra Vetere. Mantel tells of his part in it:

The host was Gen. Gohusz Szyszko who was commanding the Cavalry Force. The guests were the Gen. commanding the Canadian 2nd Corps, and the COs of the various regiments of the Cavalry Force. It was one of the best parties I ever remember. The table was laid in a summer house. The dark skies were illuminated by the glow of the explosions of the artillery fire and the air was filled with their constant thundering. Yet the guests were detached and we seemed to be in a quiet world of our own suspended amidst all this din. I shall never forget the trouble and difficulty I had in arranging it. The Brigade Major let me know about it about five hours beforehand, which is a bit late for the front line. Jeeps were despatched to get wine and a fair sized calf, cups, plates and glasses and so on. As these didn't return as quickly as I had hoped, and fearing that they might have failed in their mission, I requisitioned a calf at the farm where we were billeted. A scout car had been sent to get a butcher from Ostra Vetera and soon the calf was veal. Meanwhile the jeeps returned fully loaded with the result that the whole squadron was able to have a good meal. I think everyone enjoyed the meal, the food and the drink, and the conversation, which was mainly about horses and racing. A small argument arose between Lt. Col. Gooch and the Col. Commanding the Horse Artillery Regt. concerning the position of artillery in a mobile action.

Gooch suggested that the Arty Wallah take over his cavalry regt if he was so positive that he was correct. Good fellowship won the day and the argument fizzled out.

Next day the push to take Pesaro has to happen. Fraser reports 400 US Liberators are due to bomb Pesaro the following morning, which they do. In the afternoon C Squadron is sent in; the Germans still hold the north of Pesaro, so a destroyer off-shore engages enemy targets. Next morning just after midnight the Germans withdraw, so at 4am a new patrol goes straight in. It is then decided the Regiment will remain in reserve until a 'break into the Po Valley was effected and then [is] to be employed in the pursuit'.

This never happens. The Regiment is passed to the direct command of the 8th Army and, owing to the fact the Regiment has completed four-and-a-half years unbroken service overseas, it is decreed it would no longer be operationally sound to employ it in a breakthrough role as time is up, and it 'might have to be repatriated'. In other words, they are now homeward bound in stages.

On September 5 the Commanding Officer of the Carpathian Lancers CO, Lieutenant Colonel Zakrzenski DSO, and Squadron Leaders are entertained to lunch at Regimental Headquarters, and it is announced that General Anders, the Polish Corps Commander, has written to the 8th Army Commander expressing his great appreciation of what the Regiment has done while with Polecorps, and that they are greatly admired by his Polish cavalry regiments. He invites 1HCR to wear the Polish Corps insignia – the Mermaid Emblem of Warsaw. This compliment is much appreciated. His Majesty's permission to accept the offer is obtained, and the Regiment wears the emblem for the rest of the war.

But this is not quite the end. September has in store many smaller and shorter skirmishes, and contacts with the retreating Germans are made to the west in the Tuscan hills as they cross over once again, east to west, finally to Arezzo.

Douro, Uxbridge, du Plessis and the others are all very touched and honoured to receive the insignia of the Mermaid of Warsaw. Fraser in mid-September is in a three-tonner with a leave party to stay at the Eden Hotel, Rome, 200 miles from their front. He sees the Pope in the Vatican and as well as sightseeing, enjoys other pleasures:

> Go off at 9.15am to see Moyra Sutherland – Bruce borrows a car from 10am for the day. See the Coliseum and shop in morning. Lunch with Tony M.H. and two girls at Dell Orso. 'Sight See' all afternoon with them and Bruce C. Catacombs Pantheon, Forum. St Paul's Cathedral. Tombs of Shelley and Keats. Dinner at Eden after drink with Moyra in her flat.

Shaw, as liaison officer peripatetic as ever, is in discussion with 1/2 Punjabi officers of the KDG's 4th Indian Division, spends nights in farmhouses ('surprising lack of vermin'), searches for good wine and is unoccupied much of the time:

> Up at five to return early to the regiment. Arrived back in time for breakfast. Did nothing for the rest of the day. Walked into San Angelo in the evening with Henry Uxbridge and went to a mobile cinema there. Very bad American war film, but obtained much amusement criticizing it. Left my watch with the CIH.

Inactivity is becoming the norm. For example, October 4 and 5:

In Arezzo nothing military for me to do. In the morning got my battle frock altered and glasses repaired. In the afternoon went to an ENSA show and arrived late. Again doing nothing military. Was drinking with a few people in the Officers Club before lunch, when Peter Rapozo came in with Miss Gabrielle Brun, and sat down with us next to me. This let me in for drinks in her room before she sang, listening to her singing and dinner afterwards. It was only relieved by Teddy [Lambton] being a very drunk member of the party.

A much greater concern is affecting Ewart badly: his deep preoccupation with his ill father and when he can get home.

Wednesday, September 13. All day I have been expecting Colonel to arrive and that something would begin to be done about my going home. However it is now 7.45pm and nothing has yet happened. We fired the better part of the morning and early part of the afternoon. Not very successfully in our communication with patrols as O.P. was not very good and anyhow I don't think that they gave right map reference. Read papers spasmodically during the day but obviously cannot keep my mind off the really important thing and I have not yet made myself take seriously the obvious remedy, but I will begin now. In evening out to conference which Valerian gave. After it he told me that Ian Henderson had told him that there was no hope. I was rather indignant about this.

Thursday September 14. This morning Ian Merry came to see me. I explained position about Daddy to him. Apparently it is the Colonel's recommendation that counts in most places. I am not sure what will happen now but things look pretty hopeless. Still somehow I feel that Ian and Tony might do something between them. I feel that it is my duty to get home now – anyhow this squadron is unlikely to have to do much more work. Still God knows best. This afternoon Colonel came to see me he said that it was not worth my while making an application as it would not go through – anyhow he is signing one for me. He said the regiment would probably be home by November 1st – almost certainly by December 1st.

By contrast, for Herbert *addio a Italia* is filled with nostalgia; by now they know they are leaving, and he says his farewells.

Farewell to Mario the Roman gladiator with a heart of pure gold pursuing his Shangri-La by a dedication to sport.

Farewell to Philomena, a girl child about twelve or thirteen years old, part of a bunch of children always hovering around our cars, who one day bolder than the rest had approached me and taken me by the hand and led me across the street to meet her mother who lived in a ground floor flat: 'Mamma this is the English *Tennente* who is doing the boxing' she said. The Signora looked severe and withdrawn. Perhaps she was just hungry and worried like everybody else. But she motioned to me to sit down. There was a table with a lace cloth over it, a very upright small sofa with dark spindly legs, and two chairs of same sort. The walls were bare, but against one wall there was an upright piano. 'You play the piano Signora?' I said by way of conversation. She waved towards the girl: 'Philomena is learning,' she said. I smiled at the girl: 'Please play something?' And for the first time ever to my ears I heard Liszt's 'Consolation No 3' played haltingly as might a child learning a piece and going back over the missed notes. When it became difficult she stopped and said she was still learning it. But the nostalgia flooded into me and reminded me of my mother who played a Chopin piece so like that particular Liszt.

Farewell then Philomena with the thin face and the quick intelligent eyes but when you burst out of your chrysalis and emerge in a woman's body will you still be called by that nun's name? That surely is not your destiny!

Farewell to our little goose, so human, teetering always between dignity and ridicule. While you lived you brought a tender note to our lives, and made us laugh.

Ewart is by now stoically reconciled to waiting to see his father when he returns with the Regiment. He reports little of letters to and from home, or from girlfriends. Action in war, food, sitting it out, reading his literary authors such as Scott, fill his days. In September it is often 'did nothing all day ... still we think we are going home now so it does not matter. In fact nothing matters.' Not even the constant round of games – the inevitable bridge, the darts matches, races, boxing and netball, some rugger, the occasional dance – alleviates his unusually flat mood. But then, as Douro reports:

Suddenly we up sticks and were told to get back to Florence on a train to Naples. 20 officers in a cattle truck with their bedrolls. Anyone who had served abroad in the Middle East for four years had to be sent home. About 50% had gone out in 1940, so a lot were due to go home, myself included. It was decided that rather than try to fight on with only 50% to send the whole lot home. We were loaded into cattle trucks in Florence and went down to Naples, a terrible journey. By that time we had taken to the local wines, so we said we're not sailing on a dry ship. Before we left Florence, where they have long barrels not tubby ones, we got a long cask of rather good red wine and dressed it up as a bed roll. My manservant Pearson carried it on his shoulder on board, staggering under the weight down to the cabin I was sharing with 4 or 5 other officers. Then we sailed, about 12 ships altogether. No time in Naples.

They left on Friday October 13 on the 25,000-ton *Monarch of Bermuda*. The accommodation for the officers is very bad with nine to a cabin for two, but good for the men. The total load is 560 officers and 5,000 men. 'We are all terribly cramped,' says Ewart, 'but not as bad as the train.' He reverts straight away to playing bridge with Porchey, as he had six months before when they left Port Said.

They sail in a convoy of nine ships, three troopships and six destroyers; the food is good. Shaw doesn't find the trip much fun: 'a really beautiful day, only spoilt by the huge litter of human bodies on deck ... Also a lot of bloody women – always a bore on a troop ship.'

For Fraser, as usual, his metaphorical glass or army beaker is always half full, so he looks outwards: 'Pass Capri looking lovely ... sea calm as a mill pond ... Read on deck most of the afternoon. Lovely hot water salt bathe before dinner.'

Douro has one hope shattered, but another unexpectedly fulfilled:

I was frightfully lucky to have Pearson who had been with me since I first came out in 1939 and he stayed with me throughout the war. We'd been at sea for a day or two and we said, Shall we have a drink? Bear in mind it was local wine, shaken all around and when opened it stank to high heaven. There we were, like a lot of naughty schoolboys, not knowing what to do with this thing full of bad, filthy wine. We went to the nearest loo and bath, and emptied it – terrible smell. What were we going to do with the barrel?

Well we sneaked out at 2am and threw it overboard. It made the most terrible smack as it hit the sea and we all thought the lookout would report 'Man Overboard', so we all sneaked back to our cabin like naughty schoolboys. That was the end of my thought of drink on the way home.

After three days we joined up with a huge new convoy. I got to speak to the bursar who was friendly. I asked him where this had come from. He said it had come from the Middle East, and was picking up a lot more ships in Alexandria to go to Liverpool. I said, 'Do you think it would be possible to send a message to any of these other ships?'

They were sailing in three lines with destroyers in between, stretched over 20 miles. 'Could I send a message to ask if my wife is on one of the ships?' He looked at me in astonishment and said, 'Do you know there are 65 ships in this convoy, and it is 20 miles long with destroyers and God knows what else.'

So I answered with a little compromise, 'There is a ship behind us from Alexandria. Could you possibly send a message just to that ship to see if my wife is on board.'

A message was sent by smoke or lamp and she was on it. It was quite extraordinary that out of so many ships she was on that one. Every morning and evening we went and waved to each other or sent messages. This spread like wildfire and all my soldiers could read Morse, so there was no secrecy about what we were saying! We went through the straits of Gibraltar and suddenly in the morning our ship wasn't there any more. Our ship had dropped out! Terrible thing from my wife's point of view. We put ashore a man who had managed to get a large stock of whisky aboard and was in the last stages of DTs, and they put him ashore in hospital. We caught up again so she was very relieved.

Just as we sailed in to Liverpool I sent a message to say, 'I'll meet you in the bar at the Adelphi Hotel at 6pm.' But there was a train waiting for us, I said, 'What's happening?' 'You're going straight to Aldershot.' So I scribbled a note and gave it to a corporal in the Military Police. I said 'If you possibly can, please get this note to my wife on the *Carpathia*.' So we set off on a ghastly train to Aldershot, which took a long time as there was quite a lot of track destroyed. Took us about 12 hours. That was it. The corporal had got the note to my wife and she had gone off to her grandmother's. After two or three days we made contact.

Ewart's last entry in his diary, the first and last he ever kept, is dated October 11, 1944:

Got up this morning just before 8. Good breakfast, perhaps this is the [peacetime] chef of this particular boat. [*The Monarch of Bermuda*]. Read reports and collected money for charity most of the morning. I played bridge and Rupert, Porchey, Frankie. Lost.

There is a final note: 'Left from Naples Harbour – Friday 13th. Arrived Liverpool 28th. Went home straight away as Daddy was ill. Today is Boxing Day. I am at home as I decide to put this away in trunk.'

EPILOGUE

... the dream land
Toward which all hungers sleep,
All pleasures pass.

          Richard Wilbur (a veteran of Cassino)

October 1944. Then a young officer in the Blues, General Sir Roy Redgrave records that on the Regiment's arrival home,

> ... their casual confident manner amazed the new highly trained and technical army that had been created in their absence ... officers actually wore suede boots, coloured neck scarves, full-length shaggy sheepskin coats and had long hair. They still marched four abreast and used cavalry words of command ... It was as if a forgotten Roman Legion had at last returned from a distant province. They may not have been familiar with the new battle cries but nothing was ever going to replace their practical experience, versatility and exceptional team spirit.

Redgrave joins them to take over a troop of veterans from Lord Porchester 'who suffered from a problem with his feet and was posted to the depot'. The officers are not particularly interested in the new Daimlers issued to the Regiment, but spend their time in London 'where business at places like "Ma Feathers", who had an endless supply of girls, was brisk whilst the new Cornets had to make do with the Variety Show at the Aldershot Theatre.' Redgrave attends this show with fellow-officers, and describes a tantalising strip-tease, when in accordance with 1944 nudity regulations the performer has to remain stock-still. On this occasion, however, the plump blonde who disrobed and struggled out of her knickers, hurling them triumphantly into the air 'just as the curtain came down between her and the baying licentious soldiery' – while a flock of white doves clustered round her and hid most of her body – was undone. 'There was a loud explosion from a small blank cartridge pistol in the front row of the stalls, which dispersed the doves and we saw all we could have wished for, and more, of the open-mouthed blonde.'

Although abroad for four-and-a-half years, only a year of this has passed in actual fighting, and of those years less than six months covers that very active offensive participation in the Italy campaign. It is the very nature of their mobile and evasive tasks that they received few casualties compared to the rest of the regiments in Italy, and perhaps their deaths and injuries can be related to all the more on a human, personal level. Young though these officers are, they preserve their integrity and engage us with their essential British identity.

Apart from the dead and injured, two of their number, Ian Van Ammel and Gavin Astor, have remained behind in POW camps and end up together in Brunswick. Van Ammel keeps a prison log:

June 22 1944 (at Moosburg):
0400 visit latrine (wishy-washy diet)
0730 get up, dress, Roll Call
0800 breakfast
0830 prepare next morning's breakfast
0900 read, needlework, German lessons
1045 prepare lunch
1145 eat
1200 washing, exercise, writing, reading
1630 prepare dinner
1730 eat
1800 exercise
1900 bridge (supper 2115)
2330 bed
(Tension increases if Red Cross parcels late)

Overwhelming hunger and preoccupation with food, no distractions, restlessness, difficulty in concentrating, intense boredom.

Oflag 79, Brunswick, 23 August 1944:

The camp looked very dismal – broken tiles and glass littered the ground, the roofs had jagged holes in them and the forest and surrounding buildings were smoking still. We arrived at dusk feeling thirsty and tired but there were no lights and no water – everyone, however, plied us with cocoa and questions, and the novelty of our surroundings took our minds off our most pressing needs.

We soon settled down in the camp which is, we hope, our last residence in the Third Reich. The comparative affluence of our new companions gave us a false feeling of prosperity. We were soon on half parcels and no private parcels seemed to be arriving. This, together with the amazingly meagre German rations, soon brought home to us again that life even in an Oflag is far from achieving its promised security. However there are diversions. The theatre, cinema, gramophone concerts, play readings, and books all help to divert one's mind from the squalor and continual want of a P.O.W.'s life. I still get terribly homesick at times, but moods of depression are of shorter duration and less frequent than at Moosburg. I wish we were allowed out on walks occasionally.

The privations of the 22-year old officer deepen his self-knowledge and his compassion. He cannot understand why the ordinary German prison guards who keep him there cannot be kind or human. It seems like some awful self-fulfilling irony or prophecy; the resentment, or *rassentiment* out of which Hitlerism began, had returned, and even in the triumphant interim in which Germany had conquered every neighbouring nation and exulted in hatred and fulfilled power lust, that resentment had remained unappeased.

So was Italy, as J.F.C. Fuller observed in 1948, tactically the most absurd and strategically the most senseless campaign of the whole war, tying down resources greater than the twenty-two German divisions Kesselring moved about like pieces on a chess board? 'The situation in Italy as 1944 ended,' Timothy D. Saxon concludes, 'was fundamentally unchanged from the way 1943 had closed. German forces occupied a strong defensive position astride the mountainous north. The Po Valley beckoned to the Allies, but stayed in German hands. Another Italian harvest, the labour of Italian workers, the output of Italian factories, fed the German war machine during its most desperate days. Italy could not tip the tide for Germany, but it could feed Germans and ensure that Kesselring's forces could stay in the field through the final winter of the war.'

Kesselring himself, with a pride, even arrogance, that many Germans later show in their defeat, says the Allies 'utterly failed to seize their chances. Anglo-American commanders appeared bound to their fixed plans. Opportunities to strike at my tanks were overlooked or disregarded.' Still, there is much to say in defence of the campaign, apart from its strategic indefensibility. But nothing could justify the cost in manpower on both sides, serving as it did to strengthen Hitler's defensive death-wish, and his glory in inflicting monstrously heavy destruction during the Reich's death throes. Rick Atkinson records that after the capture of Rome, there is among the Allies 'palpable deflation', and during the next winter 'wretched deadlock ... a vast holding operation of Alexander's polyglot army of 29 nations'.

Alexander put German losses at 536,000, while the official US Army history tallied 435,000, including 48,000 enemy killed and 214,000 missing, many of whom were never accounted for. Fifth Army alone reported 212,000 prisoners captured in the campaign. An OSS analysis of obituaries in 70 German daily newspapers found a steady increase in the number of 17- and 18-year-old war dead; moreover, by late summer 1944, nearly one in ten Germans killed in action was said to be over 38 years old. Historians will never agree on the figures, even on the number of nations taking part, and ultimately German casualties in Italy remain uncertain, as they were in North Africa.

As the war moved north, Italian refugees returned home to find their towns obliterated and their fields sown with land mines. The Pontine Marshes were malarial, and nine out of every ten acres around Anzio were no longer arable. The ten miles between Ortona and Orsogna held an estimated half a million mines; those straggling home carried hepatitis, meningitis, and typhus. Two years of catastrophe were inflicted on the Italians, with untold deaths, material waste, internecine conflict and brutal reprisals as, on Kesselring's orders, ten Italians died for every German killed by patriots.

Atrocities in war are never one-sided. A particular horror story of this campaign too was the behaviour of French Colonial troops, the Moroccans or Goums, noted for their war-like looks and blood-thirsty fierceness in battle. In Lenola, captured by them on May 21, the Goums raped fifty women – but because there weren't enough to go round, children and old men fell to their savagery. The British built a guarded camp for protection, while marauding Moors who deserted in considerable numbers created havoc behind the lines, provoking vigilante retaliation. 'Either clear the Moroccans out, or we will deal with them in our own way.'

Morality declined as the war progressed. Du Plessis:

> I'll give you an instance. Some of us went on a close combat course. Dennis Domvile came back from this course and said 'They were teaching us how to burst into a room holding a pistol. The commander was really a gangster, and he said there are five people in a room and one stands up, "Who are you going to shoot first?" The answer was the one with his hands up, because he thought quickest.' If you are a civilized human being you don't think in that way. We were being monitored and taught to believe that way.

Du Plessis summarises what is to come:

> Aachen is bombed while we are besieging Pesaro. Later I remember going into Aachen in our armoured cars over rubble. I remember German civilians, women and children, not men, as the fighting Germans. I remember the look of horror as we came in, Aachen had been blown to bits.
>
> After our leave the Regiment will re-assemble at Aldershot with new equipment and we shall join in the final assault on Hitler's Germany. We shall start our last journey of this war in Holland at the Northern end of the Rhine where one branch becomes the Maas; there will be a pause before the Spring offensive of 1945. When a bridgehead has been secured farther south we shall resume our role of advance guard to various formations into the heart of Northern Germany. We shall see such desolation as I would not have thought possible, like Cologne completely flattened except for its Cathedral miraculously standing proud of the rubble all around it.

What is my conclusion? Being interested in military matters is still too often thought of as being politically incorrect by a large segment of society and therefore arcane for most people. My view is that the combat experience needs to be more out in the open, where the whole of our Western societies can benefit from the sorrow and the pride, and society's attitude toward war and fighting has a chance to mature psychologically and spiritually. We are afraid to tell each other what we really are, and the retreat caused by secular or atheistic forces weakens nations and values into narrow pacifism or obedience to fear. No people will ever reach maturity, or make sensible foreign policy, until its fighting men and women, its people and its leaders, can talk about all sides of war with equal feeling. Getting shot of regiments will never get rid of war.

LIST OF OFFICERS WHO SERVED WITH THE REGIMENT IN ITALY

Lt-Col R E S Gooch DSO	Commanding Officer
Maj E J Merry	Second-in-Command
Maj F F B St George	'C' Squadron
Maj J D Young	HQ, then 'D' Squadron
Maj N P Foster	'B' Squadron
Maj G A Murray-Smith	'A' Squadron
Capt Lord R A N Pratt	'C' then HQ Squadron
Capt W H G Gerard Leigh	'C' Squadron
Capt J G Thynne	HQ Squadron
Capt C G M Gordon	'A' then 'D' Squadron
Capt I A Henderson	Adjutant
Capt J K Doxford	'B' Squadron
Capt Marquess Douro,MC	'A' Squadron
Lt G Astor	Intelligence Officer
Lt G A Harford	HQ Squadron
Lt J H R Shaw, MC	'A' Squadron
Lt G T Routledge	'C' Squadron
Lt M L Tree	'B' Squadron
Lt E G Lambton	'C' Squadron
Lt Hon. C H Mills	'C' Squadron
Lt J W A Greenish	'C' Squadron
Lt R F S Tudsbery	'C' Squadron

Lt G W Younghusband	'A' then 'D' Squadron
Lt Earl of Uxbridge	Signal Officer
Lt Hon. E Carson	'D' Squadron
Lt J Wallace	HQ Squadron
Lt H R du Plessis	'A' Squadron
Lt K W D Diacre	'C' then 'D' Squadron
Lt H J T Carter	'D' Squadron
Lt R M Barr-Smith	'C' Squadron (Technical Adjutant)
Lt A L Rook	'A' Squadron
Lt L F Van Ammel	'A' Squadron
Lt R J G Crosfield	'B' Squadron
Lt D B H Domvile	'B' Squadron
Lt E G Wood-Hill	'B' Squadron
Lt C R H Brudenell-Bruce	'B' Squadron
Lt D J Revertera	'B' Squadron
Lt M S Crofton	'C' Squadron
Lt N L Brayne-Nicholls	'A' Squadron
Lt J C Jenkins	'A' Squadron
Lt N E Hearson	'C' Squadron
Lt G E Noble	'D' then 'C' Squadron
Lt B M B Coats	'B' Squadron
Lt J W D Ewart	'A' Squadron
Lt A Meredith Hardy	'C' Squadron
Lt A J Dickinson	'B' Squadron
Lt Lord Porchester	'C' Squadron
Lt M H A Fraser	'A' Squadron
Lt J F A Roberts	'C' Squadron
Lt J A Dent	'B' Squadron
Lt F J K Williams	'D' Squadron
Lt A G Hall	'C' Squadron
2nd Lt Hon. R E J R Watson	'C' then 'D' Squadron
2nd Lt J H Jennings	'A' Squadron
2nd Lt L H Lewis	'B' Squadron
2nd Lt D A Thacker	'B' Squadron
2nd Lt S B Woollard	'D' Squadron
2nd Lt G E Noble	'D' Squadron
2nd Lt N D Armstrong	'D' Squadron

Captain Quartermaster: E S Nicholls
Medical Officer: Capt L V Arundel
Padre: Reverend P L Richards
LAD Officer: Capt A PS de Piava Raposo REME
Regimental Corporal-Major Barratt
Regimental Quartermaster Corporal-Major Maxted,
    afterwards Roebuck

ACKNOWLEDGEMENTS

Many and varied are those who helped in the writing and production of this book and to all of these my thanks and gratitude. Second to the diarists themselves and their families, and here in particular to those I have not mentioned in my introduction: the Astor family, for permission to quote from Lord Astor's diary; and my thanks to Lord and Lady Carnarvon for permission to quote from *The Carnarvon Letters 1943–1944*, compiled by The Earl of Carnarvon.

This book would not have been possible without the generous cooperation of the Household Cavalry Regiment; my thanks to Harry Scott, the regimental Adjutant, and to Colonel Stuart Cowen the Commanding Officer, Major Paul Stretton, the Household Cavalry Regimental Secretary. I thank also John and Janine Lloyd, and Carl Johnson at the Household Cavalry Archive, Combermere Barracks, Windsor; the National Archives, Kew; the Ministry of Defence; the Imperial War Museum; the National Army Museum.

SELECT BIBLIOGRAPHY

Aitken, Tom, *Monte Cassino at War: The Political and Military History of an Abbey, 529–2000* (unpublished ms, 2003)

Anglesey, Marquess of, *A History of the British Cavalry 1816–1939* (Leo Cooper, 1973–79)

Artese, Giovanni, *La Guerra in Abruzzo e Molise, 1943–44 (the War in Abuzzo and Molise)* (Caraba, 1993)

Atkinson, Rick, *The Day of Battle – The War on Sicily and Italy 1943* (Henry Holt and Co., New York, 2007)

Beevor, Anthony, *The Second World War* (Weidenfeld & Nicolson, 2012)

Boscowan, Robert, *Armoured Guardsmen, A War Diary* (Pen & Sword, 2001)

Brooks, Thomas R, *The War North of Rome: June 1944–May 1945* (DaCapo, 2003)

Carey, John (ed), T*he Faber Book of Reportage* (Penguin, 1990)

Carnarvon, The Earl of, (Ed.) *The Carnarvon Letters: 1943–44* (private, 1994)

Carver, Field Marshal Lord, *The Imperial War Museum Book of the War in Italy, 1943–45* (Pan Books, 2002)

Como Romeo e Mario 'Le Donne Raccontano Palena dopo l'8 settembre 1943' (Bastogi, 2004) 'E Raccontano Ancora' (Bastogi, 2005)

De Courcy, Anne, *Debs at War* (Phoenix, 2005)

Debrett's Peerage 2011 (Debrett's, 2010)

Fortuzzi, Luca, Relli, Gianfranco and Benuzzi, Alberto, *Immagini dal Fronte: Italia 1943–45* (Re Enzo, 2009)

Gentile, Riccardo Vittorio, *Palena Nella Resistenza e nella Guerra di Liberazione* (Caraba, 2003)

Hastings, Max, *First Years: Churchill as Warlord 1940–45* (Harper Press, 2009)

Hastings, Selina, *Evelyn Waugh: A Biography* (Minerva, 1994)

Hibbert, Christopher, *Wellington, A Personal History* (Harper Collins, 1998)

Hildyard, Myles, Beevor, Antony (introduction) *It is Bliss Here: Letters Home 1939–45* (Bloomsbury, 2005)

Holland, James, *Italy's Sorrow: A Year of War, 1944–45* (St Martin's Press, 2008)

Hughes, Lieutenant-Colonel Dan, (Ed.) *Uniquely British: a Year in the Life of the Household Cavalry* (Tricorn, 2012)

Jary, Sydney, *18 Platoon* (Sydney Jary Ltd, 1987)

Kershaw, Ian, *The End: Hitler's Germany, 1944–45* (Allen Lane, 2011)

Lamb, Richard, *War in Italy, 1943–45: A Brutal Story* (DaCapo Press, 1996)

Lessa, William A., *Spearhead Governatore* (Undena Publications, 1985)

Lewis, Norman, *Naples '44: A World War II Diary of Occupied Italy* (DaCapo, 2005)

Maclean, Fitzroy, *Eastern Approaches* (Penguin, 1991)

Marlantes, Karl, *What It Is Like To Go To War* (Corvus, 2011)

Middleboe, Penelope, Fry, Donald, Grace, Christopher et al, *We Shall Never Surrender: Wartime Diaries 1939–1945* (Macmillan, 2011)

Moody, Joanna, *From Churchill's War Rooms: Letters of a Secretary 1943–44* (Tempus, 2007)

Ranfurly, Hermione, Countess of, *To War With Whitaker: The War Time Diaries of the Countess of Ranfurly, 1939–45* (Mandarin, 1995)

Redgrave, Major General Sir Roy, *Balkan Blue* (Pen and Sword, 2000)

Saxon, Timothy D., *The German Side of the Hill* (Faculty Dissertations, 1999)

Trevelyan, Ralph *Rome '44: The Battle for the Eternal City* (Martin Secker & Warburg Ltd, 1981)

Waugh, Evelyn, *The Sword of Honour Trilogy* (Penguin, 1984)

Wellesley, Jane, *A Journey Through My Family* (Phoenix, 2008)

Wyndham, Colonel, The Hon. Humphrey, *The Household Cavalry at War: First Household Cavalry Regiment* (Gale and Polden, 1952)

INDEX